AIR FRYER COOKBOOK FOR BEGINNERS

1500 Days of Easy-to-Make Recipes to Fry, Grill, Bake, and Roast Mouthwatering Meals. Live Healthier without Sacrificing Taste

Brandy Shawn

Copyright ©2025 by Brandy Shawn. All rights reserved.
AIR FRYER COOKBOOK FOR BEGINNERS

All rights reserved

No part of this publication may be reproduced, distributed, or transmitted in any form or by any means, including photocopying, recording, or other electronic or mechanical methods, without the prior written permission of the publisher, except with brief quotations embodied in critical reviews and certain other noncommercial uses permitted by copyright law.

TABLE OF CONTENTS

INTRODUCTION 5
WHAT IS AN AIR FRYER? 5
HOW DOES AN AIR FRYER WORK? 6
AIR FRYER BENEFITS FOR DIABETICS 7
HOW DO YOU CLEAN AN AIR FRYER? 7
AIR FRYER COOK TIMES AND TEMPERATURES 9

BREAKFASTS 12
1. Asparagus Frittata 12
2. Scrambled Eggs 12
3. Broccoli Stuffed Peppers 13
4. Indian Cauliflower 13
5. Perfect Breakfast Frittata 14
6. Healthy Squash 14
7. Egg Cups 14
8. Cheese Stuff Peppers 15
9. Omelet Frittata 15
10. Zucchini Salad 16
11. Simple Egg Soufflé 16
12. Roasted Pepper Salad 16
13. Healthy Mix Vegetables 17
14. Zucchini Muffins 17
15. Spinach Egg Breakfast 18
16. Bacon Egg Muffins 18
17. Spinach Muffins 19
18. Broccoli Muffins 19
19. Breakfast Egg Muffins 19
20. Spinach Frittata 20

SIDES AND VEGETABLES 21
21. Roasted Broccoli 21
22. Garlic Thyme Mushrooms 21
23. Spicy Buffalo Cauliflower 21
24. Roasted Eggplant 22
25. Air Fryer Mushrooms 22
26. Cheesy Broccoli 22
27. Roasted Cauliflower & Broccoli 23
28. Beetroot Chips 23
29. Broccoli Cheese Stuff Pepper 24
30. Asian Broccoli 24
31. Roasted Squash 25
32. Simple Taro Fries 25
33. Basil Tomatoes 25
34. Delicious Ratatouille 26
35. Roasted Carrots 26
36. Broccoli With Almonds 26
37. Roasted Peppers 27
38. Quick Creamy Spinach 27
39. Roasted Mushrooms 28
40. Moroccan Spice Carrots 28

BEANS AND GRAINS 29
41. Shallots Almonds Green Beans 29
42. Lemony Green Beans 29
43. Bean Stew Peanut Butter Turkey 29
44. Spiced Green Beans 30
45. Cheesy Sweet Potato And Bean Burritos 30
46. Healthy Green Beans 31
47. Risotto Croquettes 31
48. Scallops With Green Vegetables 32
49. Easy Corn and Black Bean Salsa 33
50. Green Beans With Onion 33
51. Beans With Mushrooms 33
52. Cauliflower Rice 34
53. Flavored Bean Meal 34
54. Mushroom Bean Casserole 35
55. Garlic Green Beans 35
56. Seasoned Carrots With Green Beans 36
57. Shrimp And Green Beans 36
58. Quick Paella 36
59. Salmon And Cauliflower Rice 37
60. Crispy Air Fried Sushi Roll 37
61. Pineapple Pudding 38
62. Rosemary Beans 38
63. Spaghetti Squash Burrito Bowls 38
64. Cauliflower Pudding 39
65. Gluten-Free Beans 39
66. Jalapeño Tacos With Guacamole 39
67. Crumbed Beans 40
68. Hearty Green Beans 40
69. Green Beans 41
70. Crispy Green Beans 41

FISH & SEAFOOD 42

#	Recipe	Page
71.	Creamy Crab Dip	42
72.	Tilapia Fish Fillets	42
73.	Lemon Butter Salmon	42
74.	Cajun Shrimp	43
75.	Delicious White Fish	43
76.	Salmon Patties	43
77.	Easy Bacon Shrimp	44
78.	Thai Shrimp	44
79.	Miso Fish	45
80.	Garlic Mayo Shrimp	45
81.	Perfect Salmon Fillets	45
82.	Cheesy Crab Dip	46
83.	Cajun Cheese Shrimp	46
84.	Basil Parmesan Shrimp	46
85.	Parmesan Walnut Salmon	47
86.	Lemon Chili Salmon	47
87.	Air Fried Catfish	47
88.	Nutritious Salmon	48
89.	Tuna Patties	48
90.	Almond Coconut Shrimp	49
91.	Shrimp With Veggie	49
92.	Fish Packets	49
93.	Spicy Shrimp	50
94.	Spicy Prawns	50
95.	Creamy Shrimp	51
96.	Air Fried King Prawns	51
97.	Chili Garlic Shrimp	51
98.	Pesto Salmon	52
99.	Cheese Crust Salmon	52
100.	Delicious Crab Cakes	53

MEAT 54

#	Recipe	Page
101.	Flavorful Fried Chicken	54
102.	Curried Drumsticks	54
103.	Italian Seasoned Chicken Tenders	55
104.	Quick & Easy Steak	55
105.	Simple Air Fryer Steak	56
106.	Cheesy & Juicy Pork Chops	56
107.	Moist Lamb Roast	56
108.	Pork With Mushrooms	57
109.	Tasty Pork Bites	57
110.	Steak Fajitas	58
111.	Delicious Whole Chicken	58
112.	Pork Strips	58
113.	Lamb Rack	59
114.	Beef Roast	59
115.	Mediterranean Chicken	60
116.	Herb Chicken Roast	60
117.	Simple Spice Chicken Wings	60
118.	Crispy Pork Chops	61
119.	Lemon Pepper Chicken Wings	61
120.	Dried Herbs Lamb Chops	62
121.	Asian Beef	62
122.	Delicious Cheeseburgers	63
123.	Lemon Mustard Lamb Chops	63
124.	Garlic Thyme Pork Chops	63
125.	Asian Flavors Beef Broccoli	64
126.	Easy Beef Broccoli	64
127.	Juicy Rib Eye Steak	64
128.	Stuffed Pork Chops	65
129.	Lamb Meatballs	65
130.	Flavorful Pork Tenderloin	66

DESSERTS 67

#	Recipe	Page
131.	Blueberry Muffins	67
132.	Brownie Bites	67
133.	Pumpkin Muffins	67
134.	Easy Cheesecake	68
135.	Choco Chips Cookies	68
136.	Delicious Spiced Apples	69
137.	Coconut Pie	69
138.	Strawberry Muffins	69
139.	Cream Cheese Muffins	70
140.	Almond Coconut Cheese Muffins	70
141.	Fluffy Butter Cake	71
142.	Delicious Vanilla Custard	71
143.	Berry Cobbler	72
144.	Cappuccino Muffins	72
145.	Almond Bars	73
146.	Cinnamon Apple Chips	73
147.	Moist Cinnamon Muffins	73
148.	Chocolate Soufflé	74
149.	Easy Lava Cake	74
150.	Cashew Pie	75

30-DAY MEAL PLAN 76

CONVERSION CHART 78

CONCLUSION 80

Introduction

What Is an Air Fryer?

Starting with the basics: an air fryer is not a fryer. It's much closer to being a conventional oven, and you are roasting your food more than you are frying it. The name comes from the fact that air-fried food tastes like conventional fried food and has delicious crispiness that is hard to replicate in any other way.

This is because the food is still cooked in boiling oil but isn't submerged in it. When you air to fry food, you add a thin layer of oil (usually by spraying or brushing the outside layer of the food) and then heat that oil to a very high temperature.

This not only fries the food quickly but also generates a beautiful, crunchy covering, which is something that a large number of individuals strive for when they try to make fried food at home.

Air-fried food is almost indistinguishable from traditional deep-fried food, and many things that you might love at fairgrounds and street stalls will suddenly become within your reach but more healthily.

Your air fryer gets very hot inside, which helps to ensure that the food cooks quickly and effectively. It serves as a miniature oven so that you can think of the food as baked or roasted, but because of the additional heat, it's closer to fried food in terms of its texture.

You should see a lovely golden color developing on most foods as they cook, showing that the outside is becoming deliciously crispy.

One of the great things about air fryers is that they are straightforward to use, so even if you are a beginner, there is no reason for you to be concerned with the fact that you are performing the action "properly." When you're cooking with an air fryer, all you need to do is put the food in the basket, shake it, and then wait for it to be ready.

Avoid walking away while your air fryer is cooking because of the high temperatures involved; if something cooks more quickly than expected and you aren't around, there's a risk of it burning.

It does also help to occasionally take the basket out and give the food a little shake to ensure that the air can flow evenly over all parts of it – but otherwise, it couldn't be easier! This is one of the reasons that air fryers are so popular with beginner chefs; you can make delicious food with very little input, and you don't need to be a pro to create something amazing.

How Does an Air Fryer Work?

Air fryers are available in various shapes and sizes, but they all perform the same function: air frying. They vary in features and looks; some are more advanced, some are simpler, and some are prettier, but their purpose remains the same. You have a wide variety of options to choose from in the market. Keep your needs and budget in mind as you choose, of course.

The basic features of an air fryer that even cheaper models never lack are the timer and temperature dials, which you can use to set the time and the temperature you want to cook food at. In addition, the air fryer has a built-in basket where you can put the food to be cooked and then return the basket into the air fryer to start cooking, baking, or toasting.

A few models come with additional cookware, such as a grill, a rack, a muffin tin, or thin mesh baskets for cooking small foods.

A drip tray is provided for catching oil and other food spills. In addition, you'll typically find a digital display on air fryers to tell you when to add food and when it's done cooking.

Some even have indicators that alert you when to shake the contents inside for cooking, and some take care of it.

The general idea of an air fryer is very similar to that of an oven. Plug it in, set the timer and the temperature, and then add food once it's hot. Yes, you need to preheat the air fryer before using it.

An air fryer is an easy-to-use appliance. Cooking in it becomes second nature once you get used to it.

Like convection ovens, air fryers work even better! It is countertop, compact, and space-saving. It means less work for you.

We know air fryers are mini convection ovens.

So, we can say they work the same way. Because of their small size, the fans distribute heat quickly, making the food brown, caramelized, and crispy in a short time.

As a result of its size, it does not become overpoweringly hot and does not make the entire room hot, making summer cooking almost fun!

To prevent overheating, a vent at the back rapidly releases hot air. As a result, cooking time is reduced by 20% compared to traditional frying, and energy is conserved since it heats up faster.

Oil-free frying is healthier than oil-based frying. Oil is more of a moisture provider than an essential ingredient for frying in an air fryer, and skipping oil is the first step to adopting a healthy lifestyle.

Air Fryer Benefits for Diabetics

Everyone agrees that food cooked in an air fryer has less than half the fat of the same food cooked in a deep-fat fryer, which means far fewer calories. Great news for people with type 2 diabetes or heart conditions – although all health professionals agree that you shouldn't live just on food cooked in your air fryer.

The dishes you cook must be part of a balanced diet that includes fresh fruit and vegetables.

Several studies have found that food cooked in an air fryer has lower levels of acrylamide.

This can be a cancer-causing agent and is naturally created when starchy foods, such as potatoes, are cooked at high temperatures for a long time. So, reducing the amount of starch by soaking starchy vegetables before cooking, along with shorter cooking times and less oil, is thought to reduce acrylamide levels.

How Do You Clean an Air Fryer?

Like everything that you make food in, air fryers need to be cleaned after every use. That means allowing the device to cool and then wiping it all out. You can place the basket in hot, soapy water and allow it to soak in certain foods that get stuck to it.

Do not use rough scourers or tough metal scrapers on an air fryer basket; this will scratch the non-stick coating.

For stuck food, simply allow it to soak in warm soapy water until the food becomes softened and can be wiped away.

Once the air fryer is completely cool, you should unplug the machine and use a lightly damp cloth to wipe out the inside. This will pick up any stray crumbs, bits of oil, or anything else that could cause burning and smoking inside the machine.

Wipe the outside and place it back in the air fryer when the basket is dry.

It is best not to put air fryer components in the dishwasher, even if the manufacturer states that this is safe.

The caustic nature of the dishwasher will eventually degrade the coating on the basket, meaning your food is more likely to get stuck.

It's much better to wash all parts by hand, which will help them last longer.

If your air fryer basket has a strange smell clinging to it, try soaking it in lemon juice for a short period and then rinsing it clean and putting it back in the machine.

Every few months, perform a deep clean of the air fryer and use a toothpick or toothbrush to clean any stuck crumbs or debris inside the machine.

Do not ever put the main machine in water; this will destroy it.

Air Fryer Cook Times and Temperatures

Vegetables	Temp(F)	Time
Asparagus	400	5
Beets (whole)	400	40
Broccoli	400	6
Brussel sprouts (halved)	380	15
Carrots (sliced 1/2 inch)	380	15
Cauliflower (florets)	400	12
Corn on the cob	390	6
Eggplant (1 1/2 inch cubes)	400	15
Fennel (quartered)	370	15
Green beans	400	5
Kale leaves	250	12
Mushrooms (sliced 1/4 inch)	400	5
Onions (pearl)	400	10
Parsnips (1/2 inch chunks)	380	15
Peppers (1-inch chunks)	400	15
Potatoes (small baby, 1.5 lbs.)	400	15
Potatoes (1-inch chunks)	400	12
Potatoes (baked whole)	400	40
Squash (1/2 inch chunks)	400	12
Sweet potato (baked)	380	35
Tomatoes (cherry)	400	4
Tomatoes (halves)	350	10
Zucchini (1/2 inch sticks)	400	12

Chicken	Temp(F)	Time
Breasts, bone-in (1.25 lbs.)	370	25
Breasts, boneless (4 oz)	380	12
Drumsticks (2.5 lbs.)	370	20
Thighs, bone-in (2 lbs.)	380	22
Thighs, boneless (1.5 lbs.)	380	20

	Temp (F)	Time
Legs, bone-in (1.75 lbs.)	380	30
Wings (2 lbs.)	400	12
Game hen (halved 2 lbs.)	390	20
Whole chicken (6.5 lbs.)	360	75
Tenders / Chicken strips	360	10

Beef	Temp (F)	Time
Burger (4 oz)	370	16
Filet mignon (8 oz)	400	18
Flank steak (1.5 lbs.)	400	12
London broil (2 lbs.)	400	20 to 28
Meatballs (1 inch)	380	7
Meatballs (3 inches)	380	10
Ribeye, bone-in (1 inch, 8 oz)	400	10 to 18
Sirloin steaks (1 inch, 12 oz)	400	9 to 14
Beef eye round roast (4 lbs.)	390	45 to 55

Pork & Lamb	Temp(F)	Time
Loin (2lbs)	360	55
Pork Chops, bone-in (1 inch, 6.5 oz)	400	12
Tenderloin (1 lb.)	370	15
Bacon (regular)	400	5 to 7
Bacon (thick cut)	400	6 to 10
Sausages	380	15
Lamb loin chops (1 inch thick)	400	8 to 12
Rack of lamb (1.5 – 2 lbs.)	380	22

Fish & Seafood	Temp (F)	Time
Calamari (8 oz)	400	4
Fish fillet (1 inch, 8 oz)	400	10
Salmon, filet (6 oz)	380	12
Swordfish steak	400	10

Tuna steak	400	7 to 10
Scallops	400	5 to 7
Shrimp	400	5

Frozen foods	**Temp(F)**	**Time**
Onion rings (12 oz)	400	8
Thin French fries (20 oz)	400	14
Thick French fries (17 oz)	400	18
Mozzarella sticks (11 oz)	400	8
Potstickers (10 oz)	400	8
Fish sticks (10 oz)	400	10
Fish fillets (1/2 inch, 10 oz)	400	14
Chicken nuggets (12 oz)	400	10
Breaded shrimp	400	9

Breakfasts

1. Asparagus Frittata

Preparation time: 10 mins

Cooking time: 10 mins

Servings: 4

Ingredients:

- 6 eggs
- 3 mushrooms, cut
- 10 asparagus, sliced
- 1/4 cup half and half
- 2 tsp. butter, liquefied
- 1 cup mozzarella cheese, tattered
- 1 tsp. pepper
- 1 tsp. salt

Directions:

1. Toss mushrooms and asparagus with melted butter and add to the air fryer basket.

2. At 350 degrees Fahrenheit, cook the mushrooms and asparagus for five mins. Give the basket a double shake.

3. Meanwhile, whisk together eggs, half and half, pepper, and salt in a bowl.

4. Transfer cook mushrooms and asparagus into the air fryer baking dish.

5. Pour egg mixture over mushrooms and asparagus.

6. Cook the dish within the air fryer at 350 degrees Fahrenheit for five mins, or till the eggs have reached the desired doneness.

7. Slice and serve.

Per serving: Calories: 211kcal; Fat: 13g; Carbs: 4g; Protein: 16g

2. Scrambled Eggs

Preparation time: 10 mins

Cooking time: 6 mins

Servings: 2

Ingredients:

- 4 eggs
- 1/4 tsp. garlic powder
- 1/4 tsp. onion powder
- 1 tbsp. parmesan cheese
- Pepper
- Salt

Directions:

1. Whisk eggs with garlic powder, onion powder, parmesan cheese, pepper, and salt.

2. Transfer the egg mixture to the baking dish that came with the air fryer.

3. Put the dish in an air fryer and cook it at a temperature of 360 degrees Fahrenheit for two mins. Continue to mix frequently and cook for another three to four mins.

4. Stir well and serve.

Per serving: Calories: 149kcal; Fat: 9.1g; Carbs: 4.5g; Protein: 11g

3. Broccoli Stuffed Peppers

Preparation time: 10 mins

Cooking time: 40 mins

Servings: 2

Ingredients:

- 4 eggs
- 1/2 cup cheddar cheese, grated
- Two bell peppers, slice in half and eliminate seeds
- 1/2 tsp. garlic powder
- 1 tsp. dried thyme
- 1/4 cup feta cheese, smashed
- 1/2 cup broccoli, cooked
- 1/4 tsp. pepper
- 1/2 tsp. salt

Directions:

1. Preheat the air fryer to 325 degrees Fahrenheit.

2. Place feta cheese and broccoli florets inside of bell peppers that have been cut in half.

3. In a separate dish, whisk the egg with the spices, then pour the egg mix into the pepper halves that have been layered with feta and broccoli.

4. Cook the bell pepper inside the air fryer for thirty-five to forty mins after placing it in the bin.

5. Sprinkle some shredded cheddar cheese over, then continue cooking till the cheese has dissolved.

6. Serve, and have fun with it!

Per serving: Calories: 340kcal; Fat: 22g; Carbs: 12g; Protein: 22g

4. Indian Cauliflower

Preparation time: 10 mins

Cooking time: 20 mins

Servings: 2

Ingredients:

- 3 cups cauliflower florets
- 2 tbsp. water
- 2 tsp. fresh lemon juice
- ½ tbsp. ginger paste
- 1 tsp. chili powder
- ¼ tsp. turmeric
- ½ cup vegetable stock
- Pepper
- Salt

Directions:

1. Place the entire components in the baking dish for the air fryer and combine them thoroughly.

2. Transfer the dish to an air fryer and cook it at a temperature of 400 degrees Fahrenheit for ten mins.

3. After giving it a good stir, continue cooking for another ten mins at 360 degrees Fahrenheit.

4. Give it a good swirl, then serve.

Per serving: Calories: 49kcal; Fat: 0.5g; Carbs: 9g; Protein: 3g

5. Perfect Breakfast Frittata

Preparation time: 10 mins

Cooking time: 10 mins

Servings: 2

Ingredients:

- 2 big eggs
- 1 tbsp. bell peppers, sliced
- 1 tbsp. spring onions, sliced
- 1 sausage patty, sliced
- 1 tbsp. butter, dissolved
- 2 tbsp. cheddar cheese
- Pepper
- Salt

Directions:

1. Place the sausage patties in the baking dish of the air fryer, and cook at 350 degrees Fahrenheit for five mins.

2. In the meantime, combine the eggs, pepper, and salt in a container using a swirl.

3. After adding the bell peppers and onions, give everything a good toss.

4. After pouring the egg mix over the sausage patty, give it a good toss.

5. After sprinkling with cheese, put the mixture into the air fryer and cook it for five mins at 350 degrees Fahrenheit.

6. Serve, and have fun with it!

Per serving: Calories: 205kcal; Fat: 14.7g; Carbs: 5g; Protein: 12g

6. Healthy Squash

Preparation time: 10 mins

Cooking time: 25 mins

Servings: 4

Ingredients:

- 2 lbs. yellow squash, cut into half-moons
- 1 tsp. Italian seasoning
- ¼ tsp. pepper
- 1 tbsp. olive oil
- ¼ tsp. salt

Directions:

1. Put all of the components into the big basin, and mix them together thoroughly.

2. Preheat the air fryer to a temperature of 400 degrees.

3. Cook the squash mix for ten mins after adding it to the basket of the air fryer.

4. Cooking for an additional ten mins while shaking the basket.

5. Whisk again and continue to cook for another five mins.

Per serving: Calories: 70kcal; Fat: 4g; Carbs: 7g; Protein: 2g

7. Egg Cups

Preparation time: 10 mins

Cooking time: 18 mins

Servings: 12

Ingredients:

- 12 eggs
- 4 oz. cream cheese
- 12 bacon strips, unprepared

- 1/4 cup buffalo sauce
- 2/3 cup cheddar cheese, tattered
- Pepper
- Salt

Directions:

1. Eggs, pepper, and salt should be mixed altogether inside a container using a whisk.

2. Wrap one slice of bacon around the inside of each silicone muffin mould.

3. After the egg mix has been poured into each muffin mould, the moulds should be placed in the air fryer's basket.

4. Cook for a total of eight mins at 350 degrees Fahrenheit.

5. In a separate container, combine cream cheese and cheddar cheese, then heat the mixture for thirty secs in the oven. Include buffalo sauce and mix thoroughly.

6. After removing the muffin tins from the air fryer, place two teaspoons of the cheese mix in the middle of every egg cup.

7. Place the muffin tins back into the air fryer and continue the cooking process for another ten mins.

8. Serve, and have fun with it!

Per serving: Calories: 225kcal; Fat: 19g; Carbs: 1g; Protein: 11g

8. Cheese Stuff Peppers

Preparation time: 5 mins
Cooking time: 8 mins
Servings: 8
Ingredients:

- Eight small bell pepper, slice the upper part of peppers
- 3.5 oz. feta cheese, diced
- 1 tbsp. olive oil
- 1 tsp. Italian seasoning
- 1 tbsp. parsley, sliced
- ¼ tsp. garlic powder
- Pepper
- Salt

Directions:

1. Whisk the cheese with the oil and the seasonings in a basin.

2. Put some cheese inside every bell pepper, then put them in the bucket of an air fryer.

3. Cook for eight mins at 400 degrees Fahrenheit.

4. Serve, and have fun with it!

Per serving: Calories: 88kcal; Fat: 5g; Carbs: 9g; Protein: 3g

9. Omelet Frittata

Preparation time: 10 mins
Cooking time: 6 mins
Servings: 2
Ingredients:

- 3 eggs, casually crushed
- 2 tbsp. cheddar cheese, tattered
- 2 tbsp. heavy cream
- 2 mushrooms, cut
- 1/4 small onion, sliced
- 1/4 bell pepper, chopped
- Pepper
- Salt

Directions:

1. In a container, beat together the eggs with the cream, veggies, pepper, and salt.

2. Warm the air fryer to a temperature of 400 degrees.

3. The egg solution should be poured in the pot that is used for the air fryer. Cook the pot for five mins after placing it in the tray of an air fryer.

4. After adding the grated cheese to the frittata, continue cooking it for an additional min.

5. Serve, and have fun with it!

Per serving: Calories: 160kcal; Fat: 10g; Carbs: 4g; Protein: 12g

10. Zucchini Salad

Preparation time: 10 mins

Cooking time: 25 mins

Servings: 4

Ingredients:

- 1 lb. zucchini, cut into parts
- 2 tbsp. tomato paste
- ½ tbsp. tarragon, sliced
- 1 yellow squash, cubed
- ½ lb. carrots, skinned and cubed
- 1 tbsp. olive oil
- Pepper
- Salt

Directions:

1. Mix zucchini, tomato paste, tarragon, squash, carrots, pepper, and salt in the air fryer baking dish. Sprinkle with olive oil.

2. Put into the air fryer, then cook at 400 F for 25 mins. Mix midway through.

3. Serve and enjoy.

Per serving: Calories: 79kcal; Fat: 3g; Carbs: 11g; Protein: 2g

11. Simple Egg Soufflé

Preparation time: 5 minutes

Cooking time: 8 minutes

Servings: 2

Ingredients:

- 2 eggs
- 1/4 tsp chili pepper
- 2 tbsp heavy cream
- 1/4 tsp pepper
- 1 tbsp parsley, chopped
- Salt

Directions:

1. In a bowl, whisk eggs with remaining gradients.

2. Spray two ramekins with cooking spray.

3. Pour egg mixture into the prepared ramekins and place into the air fryer basket.

4. Cook soufflé at 390 F for 8 minutes.

5. Serve and enjoy.

Per serving: Calories: 116kcal; Fat: 10g; Carbs: 1.1g; Protein: 6g

12. Roasted Pepper Salad

Preparation time: 10 minutes

Cooking time: 10 minutes

Servings: 4

Ingredients:

- 4 bell peppers
- 2 oz rocket leaves
- 2 tbsp olive oil
- 4 tbsp heavy cream
- 1 lettuce head, torn
- 1 tbsp fresh lime juice
- Pepper
- Salt

Directions:

1. Add bell peppers to the air fryer basket and cook for 10 minutes at 400 F.

2. Remove peppers from the air fryer and let it cool for 5 minutes.

3. Peel cooked peppers, cut them into strips, and place them in the large bowl.

4. Add the remaining ingredients into the bowl and toss well.

5. Serve and enjoy.

Per serving: Calories: 160kcal; Fat: 13g; Carbs: 11g; Protein: 2g

13. Healthy Mix Vegetables

Preparation time: 10 minutes

Cooking time: 18 minutes

Servings: 4

Ingredients:

- ½ cup mushrooms, sliced
- 1 onion, sliced
- ½ cup zucchini, sliced
- ½ cup squash, sliced
- ½ cup baby carrot
- 1 cup cauliflower florets
- 1 cup broccoli florets

- ¼ cup parmesan cheese
- 1 tsp red pepper flakes
- 1 tbsp garlic, minced
- 1 tbsp olive oil
- ¼ cup vinegar
- ¼ tsp pepper
- ½ tsp sea salt

Directions:

1. Preheat the air fryer to 400 F.

2. Mix oil, vinegar, garlic, pepper, red pepper flakes, and salt in a bowl.

3. Add vegetables into the bowl and toss to coat.

4. Transfer the vegetable mixture to the air fryer basket and cook for 16 minutes. Shake the basket halfway through.

5. Sprinkle with cheese and cook for 1-2 minutes more.

6. Serve and enjoy.

Per serving: Calories: 69kcal; Fat: 3g; Carbs: 7g; Protein: 2g

14. Zucchini Muffins

Preparation time: 10 minutes

Cooking time: 20 minutes

Servings: 8

Ingredients:

- 6 eggs
- 4 drops stevia
- 1/4 cup Swerve
- 1/3 cup coconut oil, melted
- 1 cup zucchini, grated
- 3/4 cup coconut flour

- 1/4 tsp ground nutmeg
- 1 tsp ground cinnamon
- 1/2 tsp baking soda

Directions:

1. Preheat the air fryer to 325 F.
2. Add all ingredients except zucchini in a bowl and mix well.
3. Add zucchini and stir well.
4. Pour batter into the silicone muffin molds and place into the air fryer basket.
5. Cook muffins for 20 minutes.
6. Serve and enjoy.

Per serving: Calories: 136kcal; Fat: 12g; Carbs: 1g; Protein: 4g

15. Spinach Egg Breakfast

Preparation time: 10 minutes
Cooking time: 20 minutes
Servings: 4
Ingredients:

- 3 eggs
- 1/4 cup coconut milk
- 1/4 cup parmesan cheese, grated
- 4 oz spinach, chopped
- 3 oz cottage cheese

Directions:

1. Preheat the air fryer to 350 F.
2. Add eggs, milk, half parmesan cheese, and cottage cheese in a bowl and whisk well. Add spinach and stir well.
3. Pour the mixture into the air fryer baking dish.
4. Sprinkle the remaining half parmesan cheese on top.
5. Place the dish in the air fryer and cook for 20 minutes.
6. Serve and enjoy.

Per serving: Calories: 144kcal; Fat: 8.5g; Carbs: 2.5g; Protein: 14g

16. Bacon Egg Muffins

Preparation time: 10 minutes
Cooking time: 20 minutes
Servings: 12
Ingredients:

- 12 eggs
- 2 tbsp fresh parsley, chopped
- 1/2 tsp mustard powder
- 1/3 cup heavy cream
- 2 green onions, chopped
- 4 oz cheddar cheese, shredded
- 8 bacon slices, cooked and crumbled
- Pepper
- Salt

Directions:

1. Preheat the air fryer to 350 F.
2. Whisk together eggs, mustard powder, heavy cream, pepper, and salt in a mixing bowl.
3. Divide cheddar cheese, onions, and bacon into the silicone muffin molds.
4. Pour the egg mixture into the silicone muffin molds and place them in the air fryer basket.
5. Cook muffins for 20 minutes.
6. Serve and enjoy.

Per serving: Calories: 115kcal; Fat: 9g; Carbs: 1g; Protein: 8g

17. Spinach Muffins

Preparation time: 10 minutes

Cooking time: 20 minutes

Servings: 8

Ingredients:

- 4 eggs
- 1/2 tsp baking powder
- 1 zucchini, grated
- 1/4 cup parmesan cheese, grated
- 1/2 cup feta cheese, crumbled
- 4 onion springs, chopped
- 1/3 cup coconut flour
- 1/4 cup butter, melted
- 4 tbsp parsley, chopped
- 1/2 tsp nutmeg
- 1/4 cup water
- 1/2 cup spinach, cooked
- 1/4 tsp pepper
- 1/4 tsp salt

Directions:

1. Preheat the air fryer to 370 F.
2. Whisk together eggs, water, butter, and salt in a bowl.
3. Add baking soda and coconut flour and mix well.
4. Add onions, nutmeg, parsley, spinach, and zucchini. Mix well.
5. Add parmesan cheese and feta cheese and stir well. Season with pepper and salt.
6. Pour batter into the silicone muffin molds and place in the air fryer basket.
7. Cook muffins for 20 minutes.
8. Serve and enjoy.

Per serving: Calories: 235kcal; Fat: 18.1g; Carbs: 4.2g; Protein: 16g

18. Broccoli Muffins

Preparation time: 10 minutes

Cooking time: 24 minutes

Servings: 6

Ingredients:

- 2 large eggs
- 1 cup broccoli florets, chopped
- 1 cup unsweetened almond milk
- 2 cups almond flour
- 1 tsp baking powder
- 2 tbsp nutritional yeast
- 1/2 tsp sea salt

Directions:

1. Preheat the air fryer to 325 F.
2. Place all ingredients into the large bowl and mix until well combined.
3. Pour the mixture into the silicone muffin molds and place it into the air fryer basket.
4. Cook muffins for 20-24 minutes.
5. Serve and enjoy.

Per serving: Calories: 260kcal; Fat: 21.2g; Carbs: 11g; Protein: 12g

19. Breakfast Egg Muffins

Preparation time: 10 minutes

Cooking time: 20 minutes

Servings: 12

Ingredients:

- 6 eggs
- 1 lb. ground pork sausage
- 3 tbsp onion, minced
- 1/2 red pepper, diced
- 1 cup egg whites
- 1/2 cup mozzarella cheese
- 1 cup cheddar cheese

Directions:

1. Preheat the air fryer to 325 F.

2. Brown sausage over medium-high heat until meat is no pink.

3. Divide red pepper, cheese, cooked sausages, and onion into each silicone muffin mold.

4. In a huge bowl, whisk together egg whites, egg, pepper, and salt.

5. Pour egg mixture into each muffin mold and place into the air fryer basket in batches.

6. Cook muffins in the air fryer for 20 minutes.

7. Serve and enjoy.

Per serving: Calories: 189kcal; Fat: 13.6g; Carbs: 2g; Protein: 13g

20. Spinach Frittata

Preparation time: 5 minutes

Cooking time: 8 minutes

Servings: 1

Ingredients:

- 3 eggs
- 1 cup spinach, chopped
- 1 small onion, minced
- 2 tbsp mozzarella cheese, grated
- Pepper
- Salt

Directions:

1. Preheat the air fryer to 350 F.

2. Spray the air fryer pan with cooking spray.

3. In a bowl, whisk eggs with the remaining ingredients until well combined.

4. Pour the egg mixture into the prepared pan and place the pan in the air fryer basket.

5. Cook frittata for 8 minutes or until set.

6. Serve and enjoy.

Per serving: Calories: 384kcal; Fat: 23.3g; Carbs: 10.7g; Protein: 34.3g

Sides and Vegetables

21. Roasted Broccoli

Preparation time: 10 minutes

Cooking time: 7 minutes

Servings: 4

Ingredients:

- 4 cups broccoli florets
- 1/4 cup water
- 1 tbsp olive oil
- 1/4 tsp pepper
- 1/8 tsp kosher salt

Directions:

1. Add broccoli, oil, pepper, and salt in a bowl and toss well.
2. Add 1/4 cup water to the bottom of the air fryer (under the basket).
3. Transfer broccoli to the air fryer basket and cook for 7 minutes at 400 F.
4. Serve and enjoy.

Per serving: Calories: 61kcal; Fat: 3.8g; Carbs: 6.1g; Protein: 2.6g

22. Garlic Thyme Mushrooms

Preparation time: 10 minutes

Cooking time: 23 minutes

Servings: 2

Ingredients:

- 10 oz mushrooms, quartered
- 1 tsp thyme, chopped
- 2 tbsp olive oil
- 2 garlic cloves, sliced
- 1/4 tsp pepper
- 1/4 tsp salt

Directions:

1. Preheat the air fryer to 370 F.
2. Spray the air fryer basket with cooking spray.
3. Mix mushrooms, pepper, salt, thyme, and oil in a bowl.
4. Spread mushrooms into the air fryer basket and cook for 20 minutes. Shake the basket halfway through.
5. Add garlic and stir well and cook for 2-3 minutes.
6. Serve and enjoy.

Per serving: Calories: 155kcal; Fat: 14.5g; Carbs: 6g; Protein: 5g

23. Spicy Buffalo Cauliflower

Preparation time: 10 minutes

Cooking time: 15 minutes

Servings: 4

Ingredients:

- 8 oz cauliflower florets
- 1 tsp cayenne pepper
- 1 tsp chili powder
- 1 tsp olive oil
- 1 tsp garlic, minced
- 1 tomato, diced
- 6 tbsp almond flour
- 1 tsp black pepper
- 1/2 tsp salt

Directions:

1. Preheat the air fryer to 350 F.
2. Spray the air fryer basket with cooking spray.
3. Add tomato, garlic, black pepper, olive oil, cayenne pepper, and chili powder into the blender and blend until smooth.
4. Add cauliflower florets into the bowl. Season with pepper and salt.
5. Pour the blended mixture over cauliflower florets and toss well to coat.
6. Coat cauliflower florets with almond flour and place into the air fryer basket, and cook for 15 minutes. Shake the basket 2-3 times.
7. Serve and enjoy.

Per serving: Calories: 92kcal; Fat: 6g; Carbs: 7g; Protein: 3g

24. Roasted Eggplant

Preparation time: 10 minutes
Cooking time: 12 minutes
Servings: 2
Ingredients:

- 1 eggplant, washed and cubed
- 1/2 tsp garlic powder
- 1/4 tsp marjoram
- 1/4 tsp oregano
- 1 tbsp olive oil

Directions:

1. Spray the air fryer basket with cooking spray.
2. Add all ingredients into the mixing bowl & toss well.
3. Transfer the eggplant mixture to the air fryer basket and cook at 390 F for 6 minutes.
4. Toss well and cook for 6 minutes more.
5. Serve and enjoy.

Per serving: Calories: 120kcal; Fat: 7.5g; Carbs: 14.2g; Protein: 2.4g

25. Air Fryer Mushrooms

Preparation time: 5 minutes
Cooking time: 8 minutes
Servings: 1
Ingredients:

- 12 button mushrooms, cleaned
- 1 tsp olive oil
- 1/4 tsp garlic salt
- Pepper
- Salt

Directions:

1. Add all ingredients into the bowl and toss well.
2. Spray the air fryer basket with cooking spray.
3. Transfer mushrooms to the air fryer basket and cook at 380 F for 8 minutes. Toss halfway through.
4. Serve and enjoy.

Per serving: Calories: 62kcal; Fat: 5g; Carbs: 3g; Protein: 3g

26. Cheesy Broccoli

Preparation time: 10 minutes
Cooking time: 13 minutes
Servings: 4
Ingredients:

- 1 lb broccoli, cut into florets
- 1/2 cup mozzarella cheese, shredded
- 1/2 cup heavy cream
- 2 garlic cloves, minced
- 1/4 cup parmesan cheese, grated
- 1/2 cup gruyere cheese, shredded
- 1 tbsp butter, melted

Directions:

1. Preheat the air fryer to 350 F.
2. Toss broccoli with melted butter and season with pepper and salt.
3. Add broccoli to the air fryer basket and cook for 5 minutes.
4. Transfer broccoli to the air fryer baking dish.
5. Add garlic to the broccoli. Pour heavy cream over broccoli, then top with parmesan, gruyere, and mozzarella cheese.
6. Place the baking dish in the air fryer and cook for 8 minutes.
7. Serve and enjoy.

Per serving: Calories: 220kcal; Fat: 16g; Carbs: 8.5g; Protein: 12g

27. Roasted Cauliflower & Broccoli

Preparation time: 10 minutes

Cooking time: 15 minutes

Servings: 6

Ingredients:

- 3 cups cauliflower florets
- 3 cups broccoli florets
- 1/4 tsp paprika
- 1/2 tsp garlic powder
- 2 tbsp olive oil
- 1/8 tsp pepper
- 1/4 tsp sea salt

Directions:

1. Preheat the air fryer to 400 F.
2. Add broccoli to a microwave-safe bowl and microwave for 3 minutes. Drain well.
3. Add broccoli to a large mixing bowl. Add remaining ingredients and toss well.
4. Transfer the broccoli and cauliflower mixture to the air fryer basket and cook for 12 minutes.
5. Toss halfway through.
6. Serve and enjoy.

Per serving: Calories: 69kcal; Fat: 4.9g; Carbs: 5.9g; Protein: 2.3g

28. Beetroot Chips

Preparation time: 10 minutes

Cooking time: 15 minutes

Servings: 4

Ingredients:

- 2 medium beetroot, wash, peeled, and sliced thinly
- 1 tsp olive oil
- 1 sprig of rosemary, chopped
- Salt

Directions:

1. Sprinkle rosemary and salt on the beetroot slices.
2. Preheat the air fryer to 300 F.

3. Add beetroot slices into the air fryer basket. Drizzle beetroot slices with olive oil.

4. Cook for 15 minutes. Shake the basket after every 5 minutes while cooking.

5. Serve and enjoy.

Per serving: Calories: 31kcal; Fat: 1g; Carbs: 5g; Protein: 0.5g

29. Broccoli Cheese Stuff Pepper

Preparation time: 10 minutes

Cooking time: 20 minutes

Servings: 4

Ingredients:

- 4 eggs
- 2 medium bell peppers, cut in half & deseeded
- 1 tsp dried sage
- 2.5 oz cheddar cheese, grated
- 7 oz almond milk
- 1/4 cup baby broccoli florets
- 1/4 cup cherry tomatoes
- Pepper
- Salt

Directions:

1. Preheat the air fryer to 370 F.
2. Whisk together eggs, milk, broccoli, cherry tomatoes, sage, pepper, and salt in a bowl.
3. Spray the air fryer basket with cooking spray.
4. Place bell pepper halves into the air fryer basket.
5. Pour the egg mixture into the bell pepper halves.
6. Sprinkle cheese on top of bell pepper and cook for 20 minutes.
7. Serve and enjoy.

Per serving: Calories: 284kcal; Fat: 25.2g; Carbs: 5.5g; Protein: 12g

30. Asian Broccoli

Preparation time: 10 minutes

Cooking time: 20 minutes

Servings: 4

Ingredients:

- 1 lb broccoli, cut into florets
- 1 tsp rice vinegar
- 2 tsp sriracha
- 2 tbsp soy sauce
- 1 tbsp garlic, minced
- 5 drops liquid stevia
- 1 1/2 tbsp sesame oil
- Salt

Directions:

1. Toss together broccoli, garlic, oil, and salt in a bowl.
2. Spread broccoli in an air fryer basket and cook for 15-20 minutes at 400 F.
3. Meanwhile, mix soy sauce, vinegar, liquid stevia, and sriracha in a microwave-safe bowl in a microwave for 10 seconds.
4. Transfer broccoli to a bowl and toss well with soy mixture to coat.
5. Serve and enjoy.

Per serving: Calories: 94kcal; Fat: 5.5g; Carbs: 9.3g; Protein: 3.8g

31. Roasted Squash

Preparation time: 10 minutes

Cooking time: 35 minutes

Servings: 6

Ingredients:

- 4 cups butternut squash, diced
- 1/4 cup dried cranberries
- 3 garlic cloves, minced
- 1 tbsp soy sauce
- 1 tbsp balsamic vinegar
- 1 tbsp olive oil
- 8 oz mushrooms, quartered
- 1 cup green onions, sliced

Directions:

1. Mix squash, mushrooms, and green onion in a huge mixing bowl and set aside.
2. Whisk together oil, garlic, vinegar, and soy sauce in a small bowl.
3. Pour oil mixture over squash and toss to coat.
4. Spray the air fryer basket with cooking spray.
5. Add squash mixture into the air fryer basket and cook for 30-35 minutes at 400 F. Shake every 5 minutes.
6. Toss with cranberries and serve hot.

Per serving: Calories: 82kcal; Fat: 2.6g; Carbs: 14.5g; Protein: 2.7g

32. Simple Taro Fries

Preparation time: 10 minutes

Cooking time: 20 minutes

Servings: 2

Ingredients:

- 8 small taro, peel and cut into fries shape
- 1 tbsp olive oil
- 1/2 tsp salt

Directions:

1. Add taro slice in a bowl and toss well with olive oil and salt.
2. Transfer taro slices into the air fryer basket.
3. Cook at 360 F for 20 minutes. Toss halfway through.
4. Serve and enjoy.

Per serving: Calories: 115kcal; Fat: 7g; Carbs: 12g; Protein: 0.8g

33. Basil Tomatoes

Preparation time: 10 minutes

Cooking time: 25 minutes

Servings: 4

Ingredients:

- 4 large tomatoes, halved
- 1 garlic clove, minced
- 1 tbsp vinegar
- 1 tbsp olive oil
- 2 tbsp parmesan cheese, grated
- 1/2 tsp fresh parsley, chopped
- 1 tsp fresh basil, minced
- Pepper
- Salt

Directions:

1. Preheat the air fryer to 320 F.
2. Mix oil, basil, garlic, vinegar, pepper, and salt in a bowl.
3. Add tomatoes and toss to coat.

4. Place tomato halves into the air fryer basket and cook for 20 minutes.

5. Sprinkle tomatoes with cheese and cook for 5 minutes more.

6. Serve and enjoy.

Per serving: Calories: 85kcal; Fat: 5g; Carbs: 7g; Protein: 3g

34. Delicious Ratatouille

Preparation time: 10 minutes

Cooking time: 15 minutes

Servings: 6

Ingredients:

- 1 eggplant, diced
- 3 garlic cloves, chopped
- 1 onion, diced
- 3 tomatoes, diced
- 2 bell peppers, diced
- 1 tbsp vinegar
- 1 1/2 tbsp olive oil
- 2 tbsp herb de Provence
- Pepper
- Salt

Directions:

1. Preheat the air fryer to 400 F.

2. Add all ingredients into the bowl, toss well, and transfer into the air fryer baking dish.

3. Place the dish into the air fryer and cook for 15 minutes. Stir halfway through.

4. Serve and enjoy.

Per serving: Calories: 60kcal; Fat: 3g; Carbs: 7g; Protein: 1g

35. Roasted Carrots

Preparation time: 10 minutes

Cooking time: 25 minutes

Servings: 6

Ingredients:

- 16 small carrots
- 1 tbsp fresh parsley, chopped
- 1 tbsp dried basil
- 6 garlic cloves, minced
- 4 tbsp olive oil
- 1 1/2 tsp salt

Directions:

1. Preheat the air fryer to 350 F.

2. Mix oil, carrots, basil, garlic, and salt in a bowl.

3. Transfer carrots to the air fryer basket and cook for 20-25 minutes. Shake the basket 2-3 times while cooking.

4. Garnish with parsley and serve.

Per serving: Calories: 140kcal; Fat: 9.4g; Carbs: 14g; Protein: 1.3g

36. Broccoli With Almonds

Preparation time: 10 minutes

Cooking time: 16 minutes

Servings: 4

Ingredients:

- 1 1/2 lbs broccoli, cut into florets
- 3 tbsp olive oil
- 1 tbsp lemon juice
- 1/4 cup cheese, grated
- 3 tbsp slivered almonds, toasted

- 2 garlic cloves, sliced
- 1/4 tsp pepper
- 1/4 tsp salt

Directions:

1. Preheat the air fryer to 400 F.
2. Spray the air fryer basket with cooking spray.
3. Add broccoli, pepper, salt, garlic, and oil in a large bowl and toss well.
4. Spread broccoli into the air fryer basket and cook for 16 minutes. Shake the basket halfway through.
5. Add lemon juice, grated cheese, and almonds over broccoli and toss well.
6. Serve and enjoy.

Per serving: Calories: 205kcal; Fat: 15g; Carbs: 13g; Protein: 7g

37. Roasted Peppers

Preparation time: 5 minutes
Cooking time: 8 minutes
Servings: 3
Ingredients:

- 3 1/2 cups bell peppers, cut into chunks
- Pepper
- Salt

Directions:

1. Spray the air fryer basket with cooking spray.
2. Add bell peppers to the air fryer basket and cook at 360 F for 8 minutes.
3. Season peppers with pepper and salt.
4. Serve and enjoy.

Per serving: Calories: 33kcal; Fat: 0g; Carbs: 7g; Protein: 1g

38. Quick Creamy Spinach

Preparation time: 10 minutes
Cooking time: 15 minutes
Servings: 2
Ingredients:

- 10 oz frozen spinach, thawed
- 1/4 cup parmesan cheese, shredded
- 1/2 tsp ground nutmeg
- 1 tsp pepper
- 4 oz cream cheese, diced
- 2 tsp garlic, minced
- 1 small onion, chopped
- 1 tsp salt

Directions:

1. Spray a 6-inch pan with cooking spray and set aside.
2. Mix spinach, cream cheese, garlic, onion, nutmeg, pepper, and salt in a bowl.
3. Pour the spinach mixture into the prepared pan.
4. Place dish in air fryer basket and air fry at 350 F for 10 minutes.
5. Open the air fryer basket, sprinkle parmesan cheese on top of the spinach mixture, and air fry at 400 F for 5 minutes.
6. Serve and enjoy.

Per serving: Calories: 265kcal; Fat: 21.4g; Carbs: 11.9g; Protein: 10.2g

39. Roasted Mushrooms

Preparation time: 10 minutes
Cooking time: 15 minutes
Servings: 4
Ingredients:
- 2 lbs mushrooms, clean and quarters
- 2 tbsp vermouth
- 2 tsp herb de Provence
- 1/2 tsp garlic powder
- 1 tbsp butter, melted

Directions:

1. Add mushrooms to a bowl with the remaining ingredients and toss well.
2. Transfer mushrooms to the air fryer basket and cook at 320 F for 15 minutes. Toss halfway through.
3. Serve and enjoy.

Per serving: Calories: 253kcal; Fat: 11.5g; Carbs: 8.5g; Protein: 26.2g

40. Moroccan Spice Carrots

Preparation time: 10 minutes
Cooking time: 13 minutes
Servings: 4
Ingredients:
- 1 lb carrots, peeled and sliced
- 2 tbsp olive oil
- 1/2 tsp salt
- For the spice mix:
- 1/8 tsp cayenne pepper
- 1/8 tsp ground ginger
- 1/8 tsp ground allspice
- 1/8 tsp ground cinnamon
- 1/8 tsp paprika
- 1/4 tsp chili powder
- 1/4 tsp ground coriander
- 1/2 tsp ground cumin

Directions:

1. In a small bowl, mix all spice ingredients.
2. Add carrots, oil, pepper, spice mix, and salt into the large bowl and toss well.
3. Transfer carrots to the air fryer basket and cook at 350 F for 8 minutes.
4. Toss well and cook for 5 minutes more.
5. Serve and enjoy.

Per serving: Calories: 109kcal; Fat: 7.1g; Carbs: 11.6g; Protein: 1g

Beans and Grains

41. Shallots Almonds Green Beans

Preparation time: 10 minutes

Cooking time: 15 minutes

Servings: 6

Ingredients:

- 1/4 cup almonds, toasted
- 1 1/2 lbs. green beans, trimmed and steamed
- 2 tbsp olive oil
- 1/2 lb. shallots, chopped
- Pepper
- Salt

Directions:

1. Add all ingredients into the large bowl & toss well.
2. Transfer the green bean mixture to the air fryer basket and cook at 400 F for 15 minutes.
3. Serve and enjoy.

Per serving: Calories: 125kcal; Fat: 7g; Carbs: 14g; Protein: 4g

42. Lemony Green Beans

Preparation time: 5 minutes

Cooking time: 10 minutes

Servings: 4

Ingredients:

- 1-pound fresh green beans
- One lemon
- salt and pepper to taste
- 1/4 teaspoon olive oil

Directions:

1. Wash and destem the green beans.
2. Put the beans in a container and sprinkle oil over them.
3. Cut the lemon in half and squeeze fresh lemon juice over the beans.
4. Season with salt and pepper and pitch well.
5. Transfer the beans to your basket and cook at 400 degrees for 10 minutes.

Per serving: Calories: 42kcal; Fat: 1g; Carbs: 10g; Protein: 3g

43. Bean Stew Peanut Butter Turkey

Preparation time: 10 minutes

Cooking time: 40 minutes

Servings: 4

Ingredients:

- 1 teaspoon garlic powder
- 3/4 teaspoon paprika
- 2 tablespoons soy sauce
- 3/4 pound turkey wings, make pieces
- 1 teaspoon ginger powder
- 1 small bunch of lemongrass, minced
- Ocean salt chips and ground dark pepper to appreciate
- 1 tablespoon sesame oil
- 1/2 cup sweet stew sauce
- 2 tablespoons rice wine vinegar
- 1/4 cup peanut butter

Directions:

1. In a pot, heat the water and cook the turkey wings for 18-20 minutes.

2. Arrange the turkey wings into a huge measured blending dish; throw with the excess fixings aside from the bean stew sauce.

3. Place your air fryer on a level kitchen surface; plug it in and turn it on. Set temperature to 350 degrees F, then allow it to preheat for 4-5 minutes.

4. Add the turkey combination to the container. Push the air-searing container into the air fryer. Cook for 20 minutes.

5. Slide out the bin; serve warm with lemon wedges and bean stew sauce!

Per serving: Calories: 283kcal; Fat: 14g; Carbs: 16g; Protein: 20g

44. Spiced Green Beans

Preparation time: 10 minutes
Cooking time: 10 minutes
Servings: 2
Ingredients:

- 2 cups green beans
- 1/8 tsp cayenne pepper
- 1/8 tsp ground allspice
- 1/4 tsp ground cinnamon
- 1/2 tsp dried oregano
- 2 tbsp olive oil
- 1/4 tsp ground coriander
- 1/4 tsp ground cumin
- 1/2 tsp salt

Directions:

1. Place all ingredients into the large bowl and toss well.

2. Spray the air fryer basket with cooking spray.

3. Add the bowl mixture into the air fryer basket.

4. Cook at 370 F for 10 minutes. Shake the basket halfway through

5. Serve and enjoy.

Per serving: Calories: 155kcal; Fat: 14g; Carbs: 8g; Protein: 2g

45. Cheesy Sweet Potato And Bean Burritos

Preparation time: 15 minutes
Cooking time: 30 minutes
Servings: 6
Ingredients:

- 2 sweet potatoes, peeled & cut into a small dice
- 1 tablespoon vegetable oil
- Kosher salt & ground black pepper, to taste
- 6 large flour tortillas
- 1 (16-ounce / 454-g) can of refried black beans divided
- 1 1/2 cups baby spinach, divided
- 6 eggs, scrambled
- ¾ cup grated Cheddar cheese, divided
- ¼ cup salsa
- ¼ cup sour cream
- Cooking spray

Directions:

1. Put the sweet potatoes in a huge bowl, drizzle with vegetable oil and sprinkle with salt and black pepper. Toss to coat well.

2. Place the potatoes in the air fry basket.

3. Place the basket in the air fry position.

4. Select Air Fry, set the temperature to 400°F (205°C) and set the Time to 10 minutes. Flip the potatoes halfway through the cooking time.

5. When done, the potatoes should be lightly browned. Remove the potatoes from the air fryer grill.

6. Unfold the tortillas on a clean work surface. Divide the air-fried sweet potatoes, black beans, spinach, scrambled eggs, and cheese on the tortillas.

7. Fold the long side of the tortillas over the filling, then fold in the shorter side to wrap the filling to make the burritos.

8. Wrap the burritos in the aluminum foil and put them in the basket.

9. Place the basket in the air fry position.

10. Select Air Fry, set the temperature to 350°F (180°C) and set the Time to 20 minutes. Flip the burritos halfway through the cooking Time.

11. Remove the burritos from the air fryer grill and spread them with sour cream and salsa. Serve immediately.

Per serving: Calories: 133kcal; Fat: 19g; Carbs: 8g; Protein: 12g

46. Healthy Green Beans

Preparation time: 5 minutes
Cooking time: 6 minutes
Servings: 4
Ingredients:

- 1 lb. green beans, trimmed
- Pepper
- Salt

Directions:

1. Spray the air fryer basket with cooking spray.

2. Preheat the air fryer to 400 F.

3. Add green beans to the air fryer basket and season with pepper and salt.

4. Cook green beans for 6 minutes. Turn halfway through.

5. Serve and enjoy.

Per serving: Calories: 35kcal; Fat: 0.1g; Carbs: 8.1g; Protein: 2.1g

47. Risotto Croquettes

Preparation time: 10 minutes
Cooking time: 15 minutes
Servings: 4
Ingredients:

- 2 garlic cloves, stripped and minced
- 1/2 cup mushrooms, slashed
- 6 ounces of cooked rice
- 1 tablespoon rice wheat oil
- 1 onion, slashed
- Ocean salt depending on the situation
- 1/4 teaspoon ground dark pepper
- 1 tablespoon Colby cheddar, ground

- 1 egg, beaten
- 1 cup breadcrumbs
- 1/2 teaspoon dried dill weed
- 1 teaspoon paprika

Directions:

1. Take a pot of medium size and include the oil, garlic, and onion; heat the dish over medium intensity for a couple of moments until it turns delicate.

2. Add in the mushrooms and cook until the fluid gets dissipated. Cool down the blend.

3. Add the cooked rice, salt, dark pepper, dill, and paprika. Consolidate well. Add the cheddar and blend once more. Make risotto balls from the combination.

4. Dip them in the beaten egg; then, at that point, roll them in the breadcrumbs.

5. Place your air fryer on a level kitchen surface; plug it in and turn it on. Set the temperature to 390 degrees F and allow it to preheat for 4-5 minutes.

6. Take out the air-searing crate and tenderly coat it utilizing cooking oil or splash.

7. Add the balls to the container. Push the air-searing bushel into the air fryer. Cook for 7 minutes.

8. Slide out the container; cook for two additional minutes, if necessary. Serve warm with marinara sauce.

Per serving: Calories: 139kcal; Fat: 7g; Carbs: 22g; Protein: 9g

48. Scallops With Green Vegetables

Preparation time: 15 minutes

Cooking time: 11 minutes

Servings: 4

Ingredients:

- 1 cup green beans
- 1 cup frozen peas
- 1 cup frozen chopped broccoli
- teaspoons olive oil
- ½ teaspoon dried basil
- ½ teaspoon dried oregano
- ounces sea scallops

Directions:

1. Toss the green beans, peas, and broccoli in a huge bowl with olive oil. Place in the air fryer basket. Air-fry for 4 to 6 minutes, or 'til the vegetables are crisp-tender.

2. Remove the vegetables from the air fryer basket and sprinkle them with the herbs. Set aside.

3. In the air fryer basket, put the scallops and air-fry for 4 to 5 minutes at 400 degrees Fahrenheit or until the scallops are firm and reach an internal temperature of just 145 degrees Fahrenheit on a meat thermometer.

4. Toss scallops with the vegetables and serve immediately.

Per serving: Calories: 124kcal; Fat: 0g; Carbs: 11g; Protein: 14g

49. Easy Corn and Black Bean Salsa

Preparation time: 10 minutes

Cooking time: 10 minutes

Servings: 4

Ingredients:

- ½ (15-ounce) can of corn, drained and rinsed
- ½ (15-ounce) can of black beans, drained and rinsed
- ¼ cup chunky salsa
- 2 ounces of reduced-fat cream cheese, softened
- ¼ cup shredded reduced-fat Cheddar cheese
- ½ teaspoon paprika
- ½ teaspoon ground cumin
- Salt & freshly ground black pepper to taste

Directions:

1. Combine the corn, black beans, Cheddar cheese, cream cheese, salsa, cumin, and paprika in a medium bowl. Sprinkle with salt and pepper and stir until well blended.
2. Pour the mixture into a baking dish.
3. Put the baking dish in the air fryer grill.
4. Select Air Fry, set the temperature to 325°F (163°C) and set the Time to 10 minutes.
5. When cooking is complete, the mixture should be heated through. Rest for 5 minutes and serve warm.

Per serving: Calories: 108kcal; Fat: 2g; Carbs: 17g; Protein: 7g

50. Green Beans With Onion

Preparation time: 10 mins

Cooking time: 6 mins

Servings: 4

Ingredients:

- 1 lb. green beans, clipped
- 2 tbsp. olive oil
- 1/2 cup onion, cut
- Pepper
- Salt

Directions:

1. In a container, combine the green beans, oil, chopped onion, pepper, and salt. Stir to combine.
2. Put green beans in the bowl of the air fryer, set the temperature to 330 degrees Fahrenheit, and cook for five mins. After giving it a good shake, continue cooking for an additional min.
3. Serve and enjoy.

Per serving: Calories: 101kcal; Fat: 7g; Carbs: 10g; Protein: 3g

51. Beans With Mushrooms

Preparation time: 10 mins

Cooking time: 20 mins

Servings: 4

Ingredients:

- 2 cups green beans, clean and sliced in parts
- 1/4 cup olive oil
- 2 cups mushrooms, cut
- 2 tsp. garlic, crushed
- 1 tsp. pepper

- 1 tsp. sea salt

Directions:

1. Bring the temperature of the air fryer to 370 degrees.
2. In a container, combine garlic, pepper, salt, and olive oil before serving.
3. Green beans and mushrooms should be stirred together once the olive oil solution has been poured onto them.
4. Cook the green beans and mushroom combination in the air fryer for twenty mins after spreading it throughout the bowl.
5. Serve, and have fun with it!

Per serving: Calories: 135kcal; Fat: 12.8g; Carbs: 6g; Protein: 2.3g

52. Cauliflower Rice

Preparation time: 10 mins

Cooking time: 12 mins

Servings: 3

Ingredients:

- 1 cauliflower head, sliced in florets
- 2 tbsps. olive oil
- 2 garlic cloves, sliced
- 1 tomato, sliced
- 1 onion, sliced
- 2 tbsps. tomato paste
- 1 tsp. white pepper
- 1 tsp. pepper
- 1 tbsp. dried thyme
- 2 chilies, sliced
- 1/2 tsp. salt

Directions:

1. Bring the temperature of the air fryer to 370 degrees.
2. Place cauliflower florets inside a mixing bowl and pulse till the cauliflower resembles rice.
3. Combine all of the ingredients thoroughly after adding the tomato paste, tomatoes, and spices.
4. Place the cauliflower combination on the frying pot of the air fryer, then sprinkle it using olive oil.
5. Put the dish into the air fryer and let it cook for a total of twelve mins.
6. Serve and enjoy.

Per serving: Calories: 135kcal; Fat: 9.7g; Carbs: 13g; Protein: 3.2g

53. Flavored Bean Meal

Preparation time: 10 mins

Cooking time: 8 mins

Servings: 4

Ingredients:

- 1/2 tsp. dark pepper
- 1 tsp. ocean salt pieces
- 1/2 cup flour
- 1 tsp. smoky chipotle powder
- 2 eggs, whisked
- 10 oz. wax beans
- 1/2 cup saltines, condensed

Directions:

1. Inside a container of moderate sized, completely blend the flour, chipotle powder, dark pepper, and salt. In a bowl of medium size, completely whisk the eggs.

2. Add the squashed saltines to another bowl. Cover the beans with the flour blend, then cover with the beaten egg. Finally, turn them over the squashed saltines.

3. Top the beans with a non-stick cooking splash.

4. Place your air fryer on a level kitchen surface; plug it in and turn it on. Get the temperature to 360 degrees F and allow it to preheat for 4-5 mins.

5. Add the combination to the container. Push the air-searing bin into the air fryer. Cook for 4 mins.

6. Slide out the container; shake, and cook for three additional mins. Serve warm!

Per serving: Calories: 134kcal; Fat: 3g; Carbs: 12g; Protein: 7g

54. Mushroom Bean Casserole

Preparation time: 10 mins

Cooking time: 12 mins

Servings: 6

Ingredients:

- 2 cups mushrooms, cut
- 1 tsp. onion powder
- 1/2 tsp. ground sage
- 1/2 tbsp. garlic powder
- 1 fresh lemon juice
- 1 1/2 lbs. green beans, clipped
- 1/4 tsp. pepper
- 1/2 tsp. salt

Directions:

1. Inside a big food processor, toss green beans, onion powder, sage, garlic powder, lemon juice, mushrooms, pepper, and salt.

2. Sprinkle some cooking spray onto the bowl of the air fryer.

3. The green bean combination should be transferred to the pan of an air fryer.

4. Cook for ten to twelve mins at 400 degrees Fahrenheit. Whisk it up once per three mins.

5. Serve, and have fun with it!

Per serving: Calories: 45kcal; Fat: 0.2g; Carbs: 9.8g; Protein: 3g

55. Garlic Green Beans

Preparation time: 10 mins

Cooking time: 8 mins

Servings: 4

Ingredients:

- 1 lb. fresh green beans, clipped
- 1 tsp. garlic powder
- 1 tbsp. olive oil
- Pepper
- Salt

Directions:

1. Sprinkle green beans with garlic powder, black pepper, and salt, then spray with oil and cook until tender.

2. Put green beans in the bucket of the air fryer, set the temperature to 370 degrees Fahrenheit,

and cook for eight mins. Flip the coin at the midway point.

3. Serve and enjoy.

Per serving: Calories: 68kcal; Fat: 4g; Carbs: 9g; Protein: 3g

56. Seasoned Carrots With Green Beans

Preparation time: 5 mins

Cooking time: 10 mins

Servings: 4

Ingredients:

- ½ lb. Green beans, clipped
- ½ lb. Carrots, peeled and sliced into sticks
- 1 tbsp. Olive oil
- Salt and ground black pepper, to taste

Directions:

1. Put all of the components in the container, then give it a good swirl to cover everything.

2. After the veggies have been placed in the rotisserie bowl, the top should be secured.

3. Position the drip pan so that it is positioned at the lower part of the cooking chamber of the Air Fryer Microwave. Transfer to an air fryer that has been prepared to 400 °F and cook for ten mins.

4. To be served hot.

Per serving: Calories: 94kcal; Fat: 5g; Carbs: 13g; Protein: 2g

57. Shrimp And Green Beans

Preparation time: 10 mins

Cooking time: 20 mins

Servings: 4

Ingredients:

- ½ lb. green beans; clipped and split
- 1 lb. shrimp; skinned and deveined
- ¼ cup ghee; liquefied
- 1 tbsp. cilantro; cut
- 1 lime juice
- A tweak of salt and black pepper

Directions:

1. Stir the contents together after mixing them inside a pot that is compatible with the air fryer.

2. Put in the fryer, set the temperature to 360 degrees Fahrenheit, and cook for fifteen mins, swirling the fryer midway through.

3. To serve, split the mixture among containers.

Per serving: Calories: 222kcal; Fat: 8g; Carbs: 5g; Protein: 10g

58. Quick Paella

Preparation time: 7 mins

Cooking time: 15 mins

Servings: 4

Ingredients:

- 1 (10 oz.) set of frozen cooked rice, thawed
- 1 (6 oz.) jar of artichoke hearts, drained & sliced
- ¼ cup vegetable broth
- 1/2 tsp. turmeric
- 1/2 tsp. dried thyme
- 1 cup frozen cooked small shrimp
- 1/2 cup frozen baby peas
- 1 tomato, cubed

Directions:

1. Preparing the ingredients. In a 6-by-6-by-2-inch pan, combine the rice, artichoke hearts, vegetable broth, turmeric, and thyme, and stir gently.

2. Air Frying. Place in the XL air fryer oven and bake for 8 to 9 minutes or until the rice is hot. Remove from the air fryer oven, then gently stir in the shrimp, peas, and tomato. Cook for 5 to 8 minutes or until the shrimp and peas are hot and the paella is bubbling.

Per serving: Calories: 345kcal; Fat: 1g; Carbs: 22g; Protein: 18g

59. Salmon And Cauliflower Rice

Preparation time: 10 mins

Cooking time: 30 mins

Servings: 4

Ingredients:
- salmon fillets; boneless
- ½ cup chicken stock
- 1 cup cauliflower, riced
- 1 tbsp. butter; dissolved
- 1 tsp. turmeric powder
- Salt and black pepper to taste

Directions:

1. Mix the cauliflower rice with the other ingredients except for salmon and toss in a pan that fits your air fryer.

2. Arrange the salmon fillets over the cauliflower rice, put the pan in the fryer and cook at 360°F for twenty-five mins, flipping the fish after fifteen mins.

3. Divide everything between plates and serve.

Per serving: Calories: 241kcal; Fat: 12g; Carbs: 6g; Protein: 10g

60. Crispy Air Fried Sushi Roll

Preparation time: 5 mins

Cooking time: 15 mins

Servings: 12

Ingredients:

Kale Salad:
- 1 tbsp. sesame seeds
- ¾ tsp. soy sauce
- ¼ tsp. ginger
- 1/8 tsp. garlic powder
- ¾ tsp. toasted sesame oil
- ½ tsp. rice vinegar
- 1 ½ cup chopped kale

Sushi Rolls:
- ½ of a shared avocado
- sheets of sushi nori
- 1 batch of cauliflower rice

Sriracha Mayo:
- Sriracha sauce
- ¼ cup vegan mayo

Coating:
- ½ cup panko breadcrumbs

Directions:

1. Combine all of the kale salad ingredients, tossing well. Set to the side.

2. Lay out a sheet of nori, then spread a handful of rice on it. Then place 2-3 tbsp. of kale salad over rice, followed by avocado. Roll up sushi.

3. To make mayo, whisk mayo ingredients together until smooth.

4. Add breadcrumbs to a bowl. Coat sushi rolls in crumbs till coated and add to the air fryer.

5. Cook rolls for 10 minutes at 390 degrees, shaking gently at 5 minutes.

6. Slice each roll into 6-8 pieces and enjoy!

Per serving: Calories: 267kcal; Fat: 13g; Carbs: 0g; Protein: 6g

61. Pineapple Pudding

Preparation time: 10 minutes

Cooking time: 5 minutes

Servings: 8

Ingredients:

- 1 tablespoon avocado oil
- 1 cup rice
- 14ounces milk
- Sugar to the taste
- 8ounces canned pineapple, chopped

Directions:

1. Mix oil, milk and rice in your air fryer, stir, cover and cook on High for 3 minutes.

2. Add sugar and pineapple, stir, cover and cook on High for 2 minutes.

3. Divide into dessert bowls and serve.

Per serving: Calories: 154kcal; Fat: 4g; Carbs: 14g; Protein: 8g

62. Rosemary Beans

Preparation time: 10 minutes

Cooking time: 5 minutes

Servings: 2

Ingredients:

- 1 cup green beans, chopped
- 2 garlic cloves, minced
- 2 tbsp rosemary, chopped
- 1 tbsp butter, melted
- 1/2 tsp salt

Directions:

1. Preheat the air fryer to 390 F.

2. Add all ingredients into the bowl and toss well.

3. Transfer green beans to the air fryer basket and cook for 5 minutes.

4. Serve and enjoy.

Per serving: Calories: 83kcal; Fat: 6.4g; Carbs: 7g; Protein: 1.4g

63. Spaghetti Squash Burrito Bowls

Preparation time: 15 minutes

Cooking time: 45 minutes

Servings: 2

Ingredients:

- 1 small spaghetti squash
- Zucchini, diced (qty. as desired)
- 1/4 onion, diced
- Bell peppers, diced (qty. as desired)
- 3/4 cup black beans, cooked
- 1/2 cup corn kernels
- 1/2 cup salsa
- 2 ounces cheese (optional)
- Olive oil
- 1/2 tsp. dried oregano
- 1/4 tsp. ground cumin
- Salt & pepper

Directions:

1. Preheat the air fryer to 425F on the bake setting.

2. Microwave the squash for 4 minutes and then cut it in half. Scoop out the seeds.

3. Rub oil, salt, and pepper all over the squash and bake it for 45 minutes.

4. Make the filling by stir-frying bell pepper, zucchini, oregano, corn, salt, and pepper for 10 minutes. Add the salsa and black beans.

5. Scrape squash flesh to make spaghetti and toss in the vegetables.

6. Bake them at 176C or 350F for 10 minutes and then broil for 1-2 minutes.

Per serving: Calories: 390kcal; Fat: 17.1g; Carbs: 51.4g; Protein: 15.7g

64. Cauliflower Pudding

Preparation time: 10 minutes

Cooking time: 30 minutes

Servings: 4

Ingredients:

- 21/2 cups water
- 1 cup coconut sugar
- 2cups cauliflower rice
- 2cinnamon sticks
- 1/2 cup coconut, shredded

Directions:

1. In a pot that fits your air fryer, mix water with coconut sugar, cauliflower rice, cinnamon and coconut, stir, introduce in the fryer and cook at 365 degrees F for 30 minutes

2. Divide pudding into cups and serve cold. Enjoy!

65. Gluten-Free Beans

Preparation time: 5 minutes

Cooking time: 10 minutes

Servings: 2

Ingredients:

- 8 oz green beans, cut ends and cut beans in half
- 1 tsp sesame oil
- 1 tbsp tamari

Directions:

1. Add all ingredients into the zip-lock bag and shake well.

2. Place green beans into the air fryer basket and cook at 400 F for 10 minutes. Turn halfway through.

3. Serve and enjoy.

Per serving: Calories: 55kcal; Fat: 2g; Carbs: 8g; Protein: 3g

66. Jalapeño Tacos With Guacamole

Preparation time: 10 minutes

Cooking time: 30 minutes

Servings: 3

Ingredients:

- 3soft taco shells
- 1 cup kidney beans, drained
- 1 cup black beans, drained
- ½ cup tomato puree
- 1 fresh jalapeño pepper, chopped
- 1 cup fresh cilantro, chopped

- 1 cup corn kernels
- ½ tsp ground cumin
- ½ tsp cayenne pepper
- Salt and black pepper to taste
- 1 cup grated mozzarella cheese
- Guacamole to serve

Directions:

1. Add beans, tomato puree, chili, cilantro, corn, cumin, cayenne, salt and pepper; stir well.

2. Spoon the mixture onto half the taco, sprinkle the cheese over the top and fold over. Spray the frying basket, and lay the tacos inside.

3. Cook for 14 minutes at 360 degrees Fahrenheit until the cheese melts. Serve hot with guacamole.

Per serving: Calories: 419kcal; Fat: 14g; Carbs: 39g; Protein: 33g

67. Crumbed Beans

Preparation time: 5 minutes
Cooking time: 10 minutes
Servings: 4
Ingredients:

- ½ cup flour
- 1 tsp. smoky chipotle powder
- ½ tsp. ground black pepper
- 1 tsp. sea salt flakes
- 2 eggs, beaten
- ½ cup crushed saltines
- 20 oz. wax beans

Directions:

1. Combine the flour, chipotle powder, black pepper, and salt in a bowl. Put the eggs in the second bowl. Place the crushed saltines in the third bowl.

2. Wash the beans with cold water and discard any tough strings.

3. Coat the beans with flour before dipping them into the beaten egg. Lastly, cover them with crushed saltines.

4. Spritz the beans with cooking spray.

5. Air-fry at 360degreesF for 4 minutes. Give the cooking basket a good shake and continue to cook for 3 minutes. Serve hot.

Per serving: Calories: 200kcal; Fat: 8g; Carbs: 27g; Protein: 4g

68. Hearty Green Beans

Preparation time: 5 minutes
Cooking time: 15 minutes
Servings: 6
Ingredients:

- 1-pound green beans washed and de-stemmed
- One lemon
- Pinch of salt
- ¼ teaspoon oil

Directions:

1. Add beans to your Air Fryer cooking basket.

2. Squeeze a few drops of lemon.

3. Season with salt and pepper.

4. Drizzle olive oil on top.

5. Cook for 10-12 minutes at 400 deg. F.

6. Once done, serve and enjoy!

Per serving: Calories: 84kcal; Fat: 5g; Carbs: 7g; Protein: 2g

69. Green Beans

Preparation time: 5 minutes

Cooking time: 25 minutes

Servings: 4

Ingredients:

- 6 cups green beans; trimmed
- 1 tbsp. hot paprika
- 2 tbsp. olive oil
- A pinch of salt and black pepper

Directions:

1. Take a bowl and mix the green beans with the other ingredients, toss them in the air fryer's basket, and cook at 370°F for 20 minutes.

2. Divide among plates and serve as a side dish.

Per serving: Calories: 120kcal; Fat: 5g; Carbs: 4g; Protein: 2g

70. Crispy Green Beans

Preparation time: 10 minutes

Cooking time: 10 minutes

Servings: 4

Ingredients:

- 2 cups green beans, ends trimmed
- 2 tbsp parmesan cheese, shredded
- 1 tbsp fresh lemon juice
- 1 tsp Italian seasoning
- 2 tsp olive oil
- 1/4 tsp salt

Directions:

1. Preheat the air fryer to 400 F.

2. Brush green beans with olive oil and season with Italian seasoning and salt.

3. Place green beans into the air fryer basket and cook for 8-10 minutes. Shake the basket 2-3 Times.

4. Transfer green beans to a serving plate.

5. Pour lemon juice over the beans and sprinkle shredded cheese on top of the beans.

6. Serve and enjoy.

Per serving: Calories: 64kcal; Fat: 4g; Carbs: 4g; Protein: 3g

Fish & Seafood

71. Creamy Crab Dip

Preparation time: 10 minutes

Cooking time: 7 minutes

Servings: 2

Ingredients:

- 1/2 cup crabmeat, cooked
- 1/2 tsp pepper
- 1 tbsp hot sauce
- 1/4 cup scallions
- 1 cup cheese, grated
- 1 tbsp mayonnaise
- 1 tbsp parsley, chopped
- 1 tbsp lemon juice
- 1/4 tsp salt

Directions:

1. Mix crabmeat, hot sauce, scallions, cheese, mayonnaise, pepper, and salt in an air fryer baking dish.
2. Place the dish into the air fryer basket and cook at 400 F for 7 minutes.
3. Add parsley and lemon juice. Stir well.
4. Serve and enjoy.

Per serving: Calories: 295kcal; Fat: 21g; Carbs: 4g; Protein: 20g

72. Tilapia Fish Fillets

Preparation time: 10 minutes

Cooking time: 7 minutes

Servings: 2

Ingredients:

- 2 tilapia fillets
- 1 tsp old bay seasoning
- 1/2 tsp butter
- 1/4 tsp lemon pepper
- Pepper
- Salt

Directions:

1. Spray the air fryer basket with cooking spray.
2. Place fish fillets into the air fryer basket and season with lemon pepper, old bay seasoning, pepper, and salt.
3. Spray fish fillets with cooking spray and cook at 400 F for 7 minutes.
4. Serve and enjoy.

Per serving: Calories: 80kcal; Fat: 2g; Carbs: 0.2g; Protein: 15g

73. Lemon Butter Salmon

Preparation time: 10 minutes

Cooking time: 11 minutes

Servings: 2

Ingredients:

- 2 salmon fillets
- 1/2 tsp olive oil
- 2 tsp garlic, minced
- 2 tbsp butter
- 2 tbsp fresh lemon juice
- 1/4 cup white wine
- Pepper
- Salt

Directions:

1. Preheat the air fryer to 350 F.
2. Spray the air fryer basket with cooking spray.
3. Season salmon with pepper and salt and place into the air fryer basket, and cook for 6 minutes.
4. Meanwhile, add the remaining ingredients to a saucepan and heat over low heat for 4-5 minutes.
5. Place cooked salmon on the serving dish, then pour the prepared sauce over the salmon.
6. Serve and enjoy.

Per serving: Calories: 379kcal; Fat: 23g; Carbs: 2g; Protein: 35g

74. Cajun Shrimp

Preparation time: 10 minutes
Cooking time: 8 minutes
Servings: 4
Ingredients:

- 1 lb shrimp, peeled and deveined
- 1 lime, cut into wedges
- 1/2 tbsp chipotle chili in adobo, minced
- 1 tbsp Cajun seasoning
- 2 tbsp olive oil
- Pepper
- Salt

Directions:

1. Add all ingredients into the large bowl and toss well to coat. Place in the fridge for 1 hour.
2. Spray the air fryer basket with cooking spray.
3. Add marinated shrimp into the air fryer basket and cook at 400 F for 8 minutes.
4. Serve and enjoy.

Per serving: Calories: 201kcal; Fat: 9.1g; Carbs: 3.6g; Protein: 26.1g

75. Delicious White Fish

Preparation time: 10 minutes
Cooking time: 10 minutes
Servings: 2
Ingredients:

- 12 oz white fish fillets
- 1/2 tsp onion powder
- 1/2 tsp lemon pepper seasoning
- 1/2 tsp garlic powder
- 1 tbsp olive oil
- Pepper
- Salt

Directions:

1. Spray the air fryer basket with cooking spray.
2. Preheat the air fryer to 360 F.
3. Coat fish fillets with olive oil and season with onion powder, lemon pepper seasoning, garlic powder, pepper, and salt.
4. Place fish fillets in an air fryer basket and cook for 10-12 minutes.
5. Serve and enjoy.

Per serving: Calories: 358kcal; Fat: 19.8g; Carbs: 1.3g; Protein: 41.9g

76. Salmon Patties

Preparation time: 10 minutes
Cooking time: 7 minutes
Servings: 2
Ingredients:

- 8 oz salmon fillet, minced
- 1 lemon, sliced
- 1/2 tsp garlic powder
- 1 egg, lightly beaten
- 1/8 tsp salt

Directions:

1. Add all ingredients except lemon slices into the bowl and mix until well combined.
2. Spray the air fryer basket with cooking spray.
3. Place lemon slice into the air fryer basket.
4. Make the equal shape of patties from the salmon mixture and place them on top of the lemon slices in the air fryer basket.
5. Cook at 390 F for 7 minutes.
6. Serve and enjoy.

Per serving: Calories: 184kcal; Fat: 9.2g; Carbs: 1g; Protein: 24.9g

77. Easy Bacon Shrimp

Preparation time: 10 minutes
Cooking time: 7 minutes
Servings: 4
Ingredients:

- 16 shrimp, deveined
- 1/4 tsp pepper
- 16 bacon slices

Directions:

1. Preheat the air fryer to 390 F.
2. Spray the air fryer basket with cooking spray.
3. Wrap shrimp with bacon slice and place into the air fryer basket, and cook for 5 minutes.
4. Turn the shrimp to another side and cook for 2 minutes more. Season shrimp with pepper.
5. Serve and enjoy.

Per serving: Calories: 515kcal; Fat: 33g; Carbs: 2g; Protein: 45g

78. Thai Shrimp

Preparation time: 10 minutes
Cooking time: 10 minutes
Servings: 4
Ingredients:

- 1 lb shrimp, peeled and deveined
- 1 tsp sesame seeds, toasted
- 2 garlic cloves, minced
- 2 tbsp soy sauce
- 2 tbsp Thai chili sauce
- 1 tbsp arrowroot powder
- 1 tbsp green onion, sliced
- 1/8 tsp ginger, minced

Directions:

1. Spray the air fryer basket with cooking spray.
2. Toss shrimp with arrowroot powder and place it into the air fryer basket.
3. Cook shrimp at 350 F for 5 minutes. Shake the basket well and cook for 5 minutes more.
4. Meanwhile, in a bowl, mix soy sauce, ginger, garlic, and chili sauce.
5. Add shrimp to the bowl and toss well.
6. Garnish with green onions and sesame seeds.
7. Serve and enjoy.

Per serving: Calories: 155kcal; Fat: 2g; Carbs: 6g; Protein: 25g

79. Miso Fish

Preparation time: 10 minutes

Cooking time: 10 minutes

Servings: 2

Ingredients:

- 2 cod fish fillets
- 1 tbsp garlic, chopped
- 2 tsp swerve
- 2 tbsp miso

Directions:

1. Add all ingredients to the zip-lock bag. Shake well and place in the refrigerator overnight.

2. Place marinated fish fillets into the air fryer basket and cook at 350 F for 10 minutes.

3. Serve and enjoy.

Per serving: Calories: 229kcal; Fat: 2.6g; Carbs: 10.9g; Protein: 43.4g

80. Garlic Mayo Shrimp

Preparation time: 10 minutes

Cooking time: 8 minutes

Servings: 2

Ingredients:

- 1/2 lb shrimp, peeled
- 1/2 tbsp ketchup
- 1 1/2 tbsp mayonnaise
- 1/4 tsp paprika
- 1/2 tsp sriracha
- 1/2 tbsp garlic, minced
- 1/4 tsp salt

Directions:

1. Mix mayonnaise, paprika, sriracha, garlic, ketchup, and salt in a bowl.

2. Add shrimp into the bowl and coat well.

3. Spray the air fryer basket with cooking spray.

4. Transfer shrimp to the air fryer basket and cook at 325 F for 8 minutes. Shake halfway through.

5. Serve and enjoy.

Per serving: Calories: 185kcal; Fat: 5.7g; Carbs: 6g; Protein: 25g

81. Perfect Salmon Fillets

Preparation time: 10 minutes

Cooking time: 15 minutes

Servings: 2

Ingredients:

- 2 salmon fillets
- 1/2 tsp garlic powder
- 1/4 cup plain yogurt
- 1 tsp fresh lemon juice
- 1 tbsp fresh dill, chopped
- 1 lemon, sliced
- Pepper
- Salt

Directions:

1. Place lemon slices into the air fryer basket.

2. Season salmon with pepper and salt and place on top of lemon slices into the air fryer basket.

3. Cook salmon at 330 F for 15 minutes.

4. Meanwhile, in a bowl, mix yogurt, garlic powder, lemon juice, dill, pepper, and salt.

5. Place salmon on a serving plate, then top with yogurt mixture.

6. Serve and enjoy.

Per serving: Calories: 195kcal; Fat: 7g; Carbs: 6g; Protein: 24g

82. Cheesy Crab Dip

Preparation time: 10 minutes

Cooking time: 7 minutes

Servings: 4

Ingredients:

- 1 cup crabmeat, cooked
- 2 tbsp fresh parsley, chopped
- 2 tbsp fresh lemon juice
- 2 cups Jalapeno jack cheese, grated
- 2 tbsp hot sauce
- 1/2 cup green onions, sliced
- 1/4 cup mayonnaise
- 1 tsp pepper
- 1/2 tsp salt

Directions:

1. Add all ingredients except parsley and lemon juice to the air fryer baking dish and stir well.

2. Place the dish in the air fryer basket, then cook at 400 F for 7 minutes.

3. Add parsley and lemon juice. Mix well.

4. Serve and enjoy.

Per serving: Calories: 305kcal; Fat: 22g; Carbs: 5g; Protein: 20g

83. Cajun Cheese Shrimp

Preparation time: 10 minutes

Cooking time: 5 minutes

Servings: 4

Ingredients:

- 1 lb shrimp
- 1/2 cup almond flour
- 1 tsp olive oil
- 1 tbsp Cajun seasoning
- 2 tbsp parmesan cheese
- 2 garlic cloves, minced

Directions:

1. Add all ingredients into the bowl and toss well.

2. Spray the air fryer basket with cooking spray.

3. Transfer the shrimp mixture to the air fryer basket and cook at 390 F for 5 minutes. Shake halfway through.

4. Serve and enjoy.

Per serving: Calories: 175kcal; Fat: 5g; Carbs: 3g; Protein: 27g

84. Basil Parmesan Shrimp

Preparation time: 10 minutes

Cooking time: 10 minutes

Servings: 6

Ingredients:

- 2 lbs. shrimp, peeled and deveined
- 1 tsp basil
- 1/2 tsp oregano
- 1 tsp pepper
- 2/3 cup parmesan cheese, grated
- 2 garlic cloves, minced
- 2 tbsp olive oil
- 1 tsp onion powder

Directions:

1. Add all ingredients into the bowl and toss well.
2. Spray the air fryer basket with cooking spray.
3. Transfer shrimp to the air fryer basket and cook at 350 F for 10 minutes.
4. Serve and enjoy.

Per serving: Calories: 290kcal; Fat: 10g; Carbs: 3g; Protein: 40g

85. Parmesan Walnut Salmon

Preparation time: 10 minutes
Cooking time: 12 minutes
Servings: 4
Ingredients:

- 4 salmon fillets
- 1/4 cup parmesan cheese, grated
- 1/2 cup walnuts
- 1 tsp olive oil
- 1 tbsp lemon rind

Directions:

1. Preheat the air fryer to 370 F.
2. Spray an air fryer baking dish with cooking spray.
3. Place salmon on a baking dish.
4. Add walnuts to the food processor and process until finely ground.
5. Mix ground walnuts with parmesan cheese, oil, and lemon rind. Stir well.
6. Spoon the walnut mixture over the salmon and press gently.
7. Place in the air fryer and cook for 12 minutes.
8. Serve and enjoy.

Per serving: Calories: 420kcal; Fat: 27.4g; Carbs: 2g; Protein: 46.3g

86. Lemon Chili Salmon

Preparation time: 10 minutes
Cooking time: 17 minutes
Servings: 4
Ingredients:

- 2 lbs. salmon fillet, skinless and boneless
- 2 lemon juice
- 1 orange juice
- 1 tbsp olive oil
- 1 bunch of fresh dill
- 1 chili, sliced
- Pepper
- Salt

Directions:

1. Preheat the air fryer to 325 F.
2. Place salmon fillets in an air fryer baking pan and drizzle with olive oil, lemon juice, and orange juice.
3. Sprinkle chili slices over salmon and season with pepper and salt.
4. Place the pan in the air fryer and cook for 15-17 minutes.
5. Garnish with dill and serve.

Per serving: Calories: 339kcal; Fat: 17.5g; Carbs: 2g; Protein: 44g

87. Air Fried Catfish

Preparation time: 10 minutes
Cooking time: 20 minutes

Servings: 4

Ingredients:

- 4 catfish fillets
- 1 tbsp olive oil
- 1/4 cup fish seasoning
- 1 tbsp fresh parsley, chopped

Directions:

1. Preheat the air fryer to 400 F.
2. Spray the air fryer basket with cooking spray.
3. Seasoned fish with seasoning and place into the air fryer basket.
4. Drizzle fish fillets with oil and cook for 10 minutes.
5. Turn the fish to another side and cook for 10 minutes more.
6. Garnish with parsley and serve.

Per serving: Calories: 245kcal; Fat: 15g; Carbs: 0.1g; Protein: 24g

88. Nutritious Salmon

Preparation time: 10 minutes

Cooking time: 10 minutes

Servings: 2

Ingredients:

- 2 salmon fillets
- 1 tbsp olive oil
- 1/4 tsp ground cardamom
- 1/2 tsp paprika
- Salt

Directions:

1. Preheat the air fryer to 350 F.
2. Coat salmon fillets with olive oil, season with paprika, cardamom, and salt and place into the air fryer basket.
3. Cook salmon for 10-12 minutes. Turn halfway through.
4. Serve and enjoy.

Per serving: Calories: 160kcal; Fat: 1g; Carbs: 1g; Protein: 22g

89. Tuna Patties

Preparation time: 10 minutes

Cooking time: 10 minutes

Servings: 2

Ingredients:

- 2 cans tuna
- 1/2 lemon juice
- 1/2 tsp onion powder
- 1 tsp garlic powder
- 1/2 tsp dried dill
- 1 1/2 tbsp mayonnaise
- 1 1/2 tbsp almond flour
- 1/4 tsp pepper
- 1/4 tsp salt

Directions:

1. Preheat the air fryer to 400 F.
2. Place all ingredients in a mixing bowl, then mix until well combined.
3. Spray the air fryer basket with cooking spray.
4. Make four patties from the mixture and place them in the air fryer basket.

5. Cook patties for 10 minutes at 400 F; if you want crispier patties, then cook for 3 minutes more.

6. Serve and enjoy.

Per serving: Calories: 414kcal; Fat: 20.6g; Carbs: 5.6g; Protein: 48.8g

90. Almond Coconut Shrimp

Preparation time: 10 minutes

Cooking time: 5 minutes

Servings: 4

Ingredients:

- 16 oz shrimp, peeled
- 1/2 cup almond flour
- 2 egg whites
- 1/4 tsp cayenne pepper
- 1/2 cup unsweetened shredded coconut
- 1/2 tsp salt

Directions:

1. Preheat the air fryer to 400 F.

2. Spray the air fryer basket with cooking spray.

3. Whisk egg whites in a shallow dish.

4. Mix the shredded coconut, almond flour, and cayenne pepper in a bowl.

5. Dip shrimp into the egg mixture, then coat with coconut mixture.

6. Place coated shrimp into the air fryer basket, then cook for 5 minutes.

7. Serve and enjoy.

Per serving: Calories: 200kcal; Fat: 7g; Carbs: 4g; Protein: 28g

91. Shrimp With Veggie

Preparation time: 10 minutes

Cooking time: 20 minutes

Servings: 4

Ingredients:

- 50 small shrimp
- 1 tbsp Cajun seasoning
- 1 bag of frozen mixed vegetables
- 1 tbsp olive oil

Directions:

1. Line the air fryer basket with aluminum foil.

2. Place all ingredients into the huge mixing bowl & toss well.

3. Transfer the shrimp and vegetable mixture to the air fryer basket and cook at 350 F for 10 minutes.

4. Toss well and cook for 10 minutes more.

5. Serve and enjoy.

Per serving: Calories: 103kcal; Fat: 4g; Carbs: 14g; Protein: 2g

92. Fish Packets

Preparation time: 10 minutes

Cooking time: 15 minutes

Servings: 2

Ingredients:

- 2 cod fish fillets
- 1/2 tsp dried tarragon
- 1/2 cup bell peppers, sliced
- 1/4 cup celery, cut into julienne
- 1/2 cup carrots, cut into julienne
- 1 tbsp olive oil

- 1 tbsp lemon juice
- 2 pats butter, melted
- Pepper
- Salt

Directions:

1. Mix butter, lemon juice, tarragon, and salt in a bowl. Add vegetables and toss well. Set aside.
2. Take two parchment paper pieces to fold vegetables and fish.
3. Spray fish with cooking spray and season with pepper and salt.
4. Place a fish fillet on each parchment paper piece and top with vegetables.
5. Fold parchment paper around the fish and vegetables.
6. Place veggie fish packets into the air fryer basket and cook at 350 F for 15 minutes.
7. Serve and enjoy.

Per serving: Calories: 281kcal; Fat: 8g; Carbs: 6g; Protein: 41g

93. Spicy Shrimp

Preparation time: 10 minutes
Cooking time: 6 minutes
Servings: 2
Ingredients:

- 1/2 lb shrimp, peeled and deveined
- 1/2 tsp old bay seasoning
- 1 tsp cayenne pepper
- 1 tbsp olive oil
- 1/4 tsp paprika
- 1/8 tsp salt

Directions:

1. Preheat the air fryer to 390 F.
2. Add all ingredients into the bowl and toss well.
3. Transfer the shrimp to the air fryer basket and cook for 6 minutes.
4. Serve and enjoy.

Per serving: Calories: 195kcal; Fat: 9g; Carbs: 2g; Protein: 26g

94. Spicy Prawns

Preparation time: 10 minutes
Cooking time: 8 minutes
Servings: 2
Ingredients:

- 6 prawns
- 1/4 tsp pepper
- 1/2 tsp chili powder
- 1 tsp chili flakes
- 1/4 tsp salt

Directions:

1. Preheat the air fryer to 350 F.
2. In a bowl, mix spices and add prawns.
3. Spray the air fryer basket with cooking spray.
4. Transfer prawns into the air fryer basket and cook for 8 minutes.
5. Serve and enjoy.

Per serving: Calories: 80kcal; Fat: 1.2g; Carbs: 1g; Protein: 15.2g

95. Creamy Shrimp

Preparation time: 10 minutes

Cooking time: 8 minutes

Servings: 4

Ingredients:

- 1 lb. shrimp, peeled
- 1 tbsp garlic, minced
- 1 tbsp tomato ketchup
- 3 tbsp mayonnaise
- 1/2 tsp paprika
- 1 tsp sriracha
- 1/2 tsp salt

Directions:

1. Mix mayonnaise, paprika, sriracha, garlic, ketchup, and salt in a bowl. Add shrimp and stir well.
2. Add shrimp mixture into the air fryer baking dish and place in the air fryer.
3. Cook at 325 F for 8 minutes. Stir halfway through.
4. Serve and enjoy.

Per serving: Calories: 185kcal; Fat: 5g; Carbs: 6g; Protein: 25g

96. Air Fried King Prawns

Preparation time: 10 minutes

Cooking time: 6 minutes

Servings: 4

Ingredients:

- 12 king prawns
- 1 tbsp vinegar
- 1 tbsp ketchup
- 3 tbsp mayonnaise
- 1/2 tsp pepper
- 1 tsp chili powder
- 1 tsp red chili flakes
- 1/2 tsp sea salt

Directions:

1. Preheat the air fryer to 350 F.
2. Spray the air fryer basket with cooking spray.
3. Add prawns, chili flakes, chili powder, pepper, and salt to the bowl and toss well.
4. Transfer the shrimp to the air fryer basket and cook for 6 minutes.
5. In a small bowl, mix mayonnaise, ketchup, and vinegar.
6. Serve with mayo mixture, and enjoy.

Per serving: Calories: 130kcal; Fat: 5g; Carbs: 5g; Protein: 15g

97. Chili Garlic Shrimp

Preparation time: 10 minutes

Cooking time: 7 minutes

Servings: 4

Ingredients:

- 1 lb shrimp, peeled and deveined
- 1 tbsp olive oil
- 1 lemon, sliced
- 1 red chili pepper, sliced
- 1/2 tsp garlic powder
- Pepper
- Salt

Directions:

1. Preheat the air fryer to 400 F.

2. Spray the air fryer basket with cooking spray.

3. Add all ingredients into the bowl and toss well.

4. Add shrimp into the air fryer basket and cook for 5 minutes. Shake the basket twice.

5. Serve and enjoy.

Per serving: Calories: 170kcal; Fat: 5g; Carbs: 3g; Protein: 25g

98. Pesto Salmon

Preparation time: 10 minutes

Cooking time: 16 minutes

Servings: 4

Ingredients:

- 25 oz salmon fillet
- 1 tbsp green pesto
- 1 cup mayonnaise
- 1/2 oz olive oil
- 1 lb. fresh spinach
- 2 oz parmesan cheese, grated
- Pepper
- Salt

Directions:

1. Preheat the air fryer to 370 F.

2. Spray the air fryer basket with cooking spray.

3. Season salmon fillet with pepper and salt and place into the air fryer basket.

4. Mix mayonnaise, parmesan cheese, and pesto in a bowl and spread over the salmon fillet.

5. Cook salmon for 14-16 minutes.

6. Meanwhile, in a pan, sauté spinach with olive oil until spinach is wilted, about 2-3 minutes. Season with pepper and salt.

7. Transfer spinach to a serving plate and top with cooked salmon.

8. Serve and enjoy.

Per serving: Calories: 545kcal; Fat: 39.6g; Carbs: 9.5g; Protein: 43g

99. Cheese Crust Salmon

Preparation time: 10 minutes

Cooking time: 10 minutes

Servings: 5

Ingredients:

- 5 salmon fillets
- 1 tsp Italian seasoning
- 2 garlic cloves, minced
- 1 cup parmesan cheese, shredded
- 1 tsp paprika
- 1 tbsp olive oil
- 1/4 cup fresh parsley, chopped
- Pepper
- Salt

Directions:

1. Preheat the air fryer to 425 F.

2. Add salmon, seasoning, and olive oil to the bowl and mix well.

3. Place the salmon fillet into the air fryer basket.

4. In another bowl, mix cheese, garlic, and parsley.

5. Sprinkle cheese mixture on top of salmon and cook for 10 minutes.

6. Serve and enjoy.

Per serving: Calories: 333kcal; Fat: 18g; Carbs: 2g; Protein: 40g

100. Delicious Crab Cakes

Preparation time: 10 mins

Cooking time: 10 mins

Servings: 4

Ingredients:

- 8 oz. crab meat
- 2 tbsps. butter, liquified
- 2 tsps. Dijon mustard
- 1 tbsp. mayonnaise
- 1 egg, casually crushed
- 1/2 tsp. old bay seasoning
- 1 green onion, cut
- 2 tbsps. parsley, sliced
- 1/4 cup almond flour
- 1/4 tsp. pepper
- 1/2 tsp. salt

Directions:

1. Bring all ingredients except butter into a mixing bowl, then mix until well combined.

2. Make four equal shapes of patties from the mix and put them on a lined parchment paper.

3. Place the plate in the fridge for thirty mins.

4. Drizzle the air fryer basket with cooking spray.

5. Brush melted butter on both sides of the crab patties.

6. Place crab patties in an air fryer basket and cook for ten mins at 350 F.

7. Turn patties halfway through.

8. Serve and enjoy.

Per serving: Calories: 136kcal; Fat: 12.6g; Carbs: 4.1g; Protein: 10.3g

Meat

101. Flavorful Fried Chicken

Preparation time: 10 mins

Cooking time: 40 mins

Servings: 10

Ingredients:

- 5 lbs. chicken, around ten parts
- 1 tbsp. coconut oil
- 2 1/2 tsps. white pepper
- 1 tsp. ground ginger
- 1 1/2 tsps. garlic salt
- 1 tbsp. paprika
- 1 tsp. dried mustard
- 1 tsp. pepper
- 1 tsp. celery salt
- 1/3 tsp. oregano
- 1/2 tsp. basil
- 1/2 tsp. thyme
- 2 cups pork rinds, crumpled
- 1 tbsp. vinegar
- 1 cup sour almond milk
- 1/2 tsp. salt

Directions:

1. Add chicken to a large mixing bowl.
2. Include milk and vinegar over chicken and put in the refrigerator for two hrs.
3. Combine pork rinds, white pepper, ginger, garlic salt, paprika, mustard, pepper, celery salt, oregano, basil, thyme, and salt in a shallow dish.
4. Coat the air fryer basket with coconut oil.
5. Coat each chicken piece with pork rind mixture and place on a plate.
6. Place half-coated chicken in the air fryer basket.
7. Cook chicken at 360 F for ten mins, then turn chicken to another side and cook for ten mins additional or till internal temperature reaches 165º F.
8. Cook the remaining chicken using the same method.
9. Serve and have fun with it.

Per serving: Calories: 539kcal; Fat: 37g; Carbs: 1g; Protein: 45g

102. Curried Drumsticks

Preparation time: 10 mins

Cooking time: 22 mins

Servings: 2

Ingredients:

- 2 turkey drumsticks
- 1/3 cup coconut milk
- 1 1/2 tbsps. ginger, minced
- 1/4 tsp. cayenne pepper
- 2 tbsps. red curry paste
- 1/4 tsp. pepper
- 1 tsp. kosher salt

Directions:

1. Include the entire components into the bowl and stir to coat. Place in refrigerator overnight.
2. Sprinkle the air fryer basket with cooking spray.

3. Put marinated drumsticks in the air fryer basket and cook at 390 F for twenty-two mins.

4. Serve and have fun with it.

Per serving: Calories: 279kcal; Fat: 18g; Carbs: 8g; Protein: 20g

103. Italian Seasoned Chicken Tenders

Preparation time: 10 mins

Cooking time: 10 mins

Servings: 2

Ingredients:

- 2 eggs, lightly beaten
- 1 1/2 lbs. chicken tenders
- 1/2 tsp. onion powder
- 1/2 tsp. garlic powder
- 1 tsp. paprika
- 1 tsp. Italian seasoning
- 2 tbsps. ground flax seed
- 1 cup almond flour
- 1/2 tsp. pepper
- 1 tsp. sea salt

Directions:

1. Preheat the air fryer to 400 F.

2. Season chicken with pepper and salt.

3. In a medium bowl, whisk eggs to combine.

4. Combine almond flour, all seasonings, and flaxseed in a shallow dish.

5. Dip chicken into the egg, then coats with almond flour mixture and place on a plate.

6. Spray the air fryer basket with cooking spray.

7. Place half chicken tenders in an air fryer basket and cook for ten mins. Turn halfway through.

8. Cook the remaining chicken tenders using the same steps.

9. Serve and enjoy.

Per serving: Calories: 315kcal; Fat: 21g; Carbs: 12g; Protein: 17g

104. Quick & Easy Steak

Preparation time: 10 mins

Cooking time: 7 mins

Servings: 2

Ingredients:

- 12 oz. steaks
- 1/2 tbsp. unsweetened cocoa powder
- 1 tbsp. Montreal steak seasoning
- 1 tsp. liquid smoke
- 1 tbsp. soy sauce
- Pepper
- Salt

Directions:

1. Include steak, liquid smoke, and soy sauce in a zip-lock bag and shake thoroughly.

2. Season steak with seasonings and place in the refrigerator overnight.

3. Put marinated steak in an air fryer basket and cook at 375 F for five mins.

4. Turn the steak to another side and cook for additional two mins

5. Serve and enjoy.

Per serving: Calories: 356kcal; Fat: 8.7g; Carbs: 1.4g; Protein: 62.2g

105. Simple Air Fryer Steak

Preparation time: 10 mins

Cooking time: 18 mins

Servings: 2

Ingredients:

- 12 oz. steaks, 3/4-inch thick
- 1 tsp. garlic powder
- 1 tsp. olive oil
- Pepper
- Salt

Directions:

1. Coat steaks with oil and season with garlic powder, pepper, and salt.
2. Preheat the air fryer to 400 F.
3. Place steaks in an air fryer basket and cook for fifteen to eighteen mins. Turn halfway through.
4. Serve and enjoy.

Per serving: Calories: 363kcal; Fat: 5g; Carbs: 1.1g; Protein: 61.7g

106. Cheesy & Juicy Pork Chops

Preparation time: 10 mins

Cooking time: 8 mins

Servings: 2

Ingredients:

- 4 pork chops
- 1/4 cup cheddar cheese, tattered
- 1/2 tsp. garlic powder
- 1/2 tsp. salt

Directions:

1. Preheat the air fryer to 350 F.
2. Rub pork chops with garlic powder and salt and place in the air fryer basket.
3. Cook pork chops for four mins.
4. Turn pork chops to another side and cook for two mins.
5. Include cheese on top of pork chops and cook for additional two mins.
6. Serve and enjoy.

Per serving: Calories: 465kcal; Fat: 22g; Carbs: 2g; Protein: 61g

107. Moist Lamb Roast

Preparation time: 5 mins

Cooking time: 1 hr 30 mins

Servings: 4

Ingredients:

- 2 1/2 lbs. lamb leg roast
- 1 tbsp. dried rosemary
- 3 garlic cloves, cut
- 1 tbsp. olive oil
- Pepper
- Salt

Directions:

1. Make small cuts of meat using a sharp knife.
2. Poke garlic slices into the cuts. Season meat with pepper and salt.
3. Mix oil and rosemary and rub over the meat.
4. Place meat into the air fryer and cook at 400 F for fifteen mins.

5. Turn the temperature to 320 F for 1 hour and fifteen mins.

6. Serve and enjoy.

Per serving: Calories: 595kcal; Fat: 25g; Carbs: 2g; Protein: 85g

108. Pork With Mushrooms

Preparation time: 10 mins

Cooking time: 18 mins

Servings: 4

Ingredients:

- 1 lb. pork chops, rinsed and pat dry
- 1/2 tsp. garlic powder
- 1 tsp. soy sauce
- 2 tbsps. butter, liquified
- 8 oz. mushrooms, split
- Pepper
- Salt

Directions:

1. Preheat the air fryer to 400 F.

2. Cut pork chops into 3/4-inch cubes and place in a large mixing bowl.

3. Add the remaining ingredients into the bowl and toss well.

4. Transfer the pork and mushroom mixture to the air fryer basket and cook for fifteen to eighteen mins. Shake the basket midway through.

5. Serve and enjoy.

Per serving: Calories: 428kcal; Fat: 7g; Carbs: 2.2g; Protein: 27.5g

109. Tasty Pork Bites

Preparation time: 10 mins

Cooking time: 21 mins

Servings: 6

Ingredients:

- 2 eggs, lightly beaten
- 1 lb. pork tenderloin, cut into cubes
- ¼ cup almond flour
- ½ tsp. ground coriander
- ½ tsp. paprika
- ½ tsp. lemon zest
- ½ tsp. kosher salt

Directions:

1. In a shallow bowl, whisk eggs.

2. Mix almond flour, coriander, paprika, lemon zest, and salt in a shallow dish.

3. Dip each pork cube in egg, then coat with almond flour mixture.

4. Preheat the air fryer to 365 F.

5. Spray the air fryer basket with cooking spray.

6. Include coated pork cubes into the air fryer basket and cook for fourteen mins.

7. Turn pork cubes to another side and cook for a further seven mins.

8. Serve and enjoy.

Per serving: Calories: 135kcal; Fat: 4g; Carbs: 0.2g; Protein: 21g

110. Steak Fajitas

Preparation time: 10 mins

Cooking time: 15 mins

Servings: 6

Ingredients:

- 1 lb. steak, cut
- 1 tbsp. olive oil
- 1 tbsp. fajita seasoning, gluten-free
- 1/2 cup onion, cut
- 3 bell peppers, cut

Directions:

1. Line the air fryer basket with aluminum foil.
2. Add all ingredients large bowl and toss until well coated.
3. Transfer the fajita mixture to the air fryer basket and cook at 390 F for five mins.
4. Toss and cook for a further five to ten mins.
5. Serve and enjoy.

Per serving: Calories: 304kcal; Fat: 17g; Carbs: 15g; Protein: 22g

111. Delicious Whole Chicken

Preparation time: 10 minutes

Cooking time: 50 minutes

Servings: 4

Ingredients:

- 3 lbs. whole chicken, remove giblets and pat dry chicken
- 1 tsp Italian seasoning
- 1/2 tsp garlic powder
- 1/2 tsp onion powder
- 1/4 tsp paprika
- 1/4 tsp pepper
- 1 1/2 tsp salt

Directions:

1. Mix Italian seasoning, garlic powder, onion powder, paprika, pepper, and salt in a small bowl.
2. Rub spice mixture from inside and outside of the chicken.
3. Place chicken breast side down in the air fryer basket.
4. Roast chicken for 30 minutes at 360 F.
5. Turn the chicken and roast for 20 minutes more, or the internal temperature of the chicken reaches 165 F.
6. Serve and enjoy.

Per serving: Calories: 356kcal; Fat: 25g; Carbs: 1g; Protein: 30g

112. Pork Strips

Preparation time: 10 minutes

Cooking time: 10 minutes

Servings: 2

Ingredients:

- 4 pork loin chops
- 1 tbsp swerve
- 1 tbsp soy sauce
- 1/8 tsp ground ginger
- 1 garlic clove, chopped
- 1/2 tsp balsamic vinegar

Directions:

1. Tenderize meat and season with pepper and salt.

2. In a bowl, mix sweetener, soy sauce, and vinegar. Add ginger and garlic and set aside.

3. Add pork chops into the marinade mixture and marinate for 2 hours.

4. Preheat the air fryer to 350 F.

5. Add marinated meat into the air fryer and cook for 5 minutes on each side.

6. Cut into strips and serve.

Per serving: Calories: 551kcal; Fat: 39.8g; Carbs: 9.9g; Protein: 36.6g

113. Lamb Rack

Preparation time: 10 minutes
Cooking time: 30 minutes
Servings: 6
Ingredients:

- 1 egg, lightly beaten
- 1 tbsp fresh thyme, chopped
- 1 3/4 lbs. rack of lamb
- 1 tbsp fresh rosemary, chopped
- 1 tbsp olive oil
- 2 garlic cloves, chopped
- Pepper
- Salt

Directions:

1. Mix oil and garlic.

2. Brush the oil and garlic mixture over the rack of lamb. Season with pepper and salt.

3. Preheat the air fryer to 210 F.

4. Mix thyme and rosemary.

5. Coat lamb with egg, then with herb mixture.

6. Place the lamb rack in the air fryer basket and cook for 25 minutes.

7. Turn the temperature to 390 F and cook for 5 minutes more.

8. Serve and enjoy.

Per serving: Calories: 255kcal; Fat: 15g; Carbs: 1g; Protein: 29g

114. Beef Roast

Preparation time: 10 minutes
Cooking time: 35 minutes
Servings: 7
Ingredients:

- 2 lbs. beef roast
- 1 tbsp olive oil
- 1 tsp thyme
- 2 tsp garlic powder
- 1/4 tsp pepper
- 1 tbsp kosher salt

Directions:

1. Coat roast with olive oil.

2. Mix thyme, garlic powder, pepper, and salt and rub all over the roast.

3. Place roast into the air fryer basket and cook at 400 F for 20 minutes.

4. Spray roast with cooking spray and cook for 15 minutes more.

5. Slice and serve.

Per serving: Calories: 238kcal; Fat: 13g; Carbs: 1g; Protein: 25g

115. Mediterranean Chicken

Preparation time: 10 minutes

Cooking time: 35 minutes

Servings: 6

Ingredients:

- 4 lbs. whole chicken, cut into pieces
- 2 tsp ground sumac
- 2 garlic cloves, minced
- 2 lemons, sliced
- 2 tbsp olive oil
- 1 tsp lemon zest
- 2 tsp kosher salt

Directions:

1. Rub chicken with oil, sumac, lemon zest, and salt. Place in the refrigerator for 2-3 hours.
2. Add lemon sliced into the air fryer basket top with marinated chicken.
3. Cook at 350 for 35 minutes.
4. Serve and enjoy.

Per serving: Calories: 616kcal; Fat: 27g; Carbs: 0.4g; Protein: 87g

116. Herb Chicken Roast

Preparation time: 10 minutes

Cooking time: 25 minutes

Servings: 2

Ingredients:

- 10 oz chicken breast
- 1/4 tsp dried thyme
- 1/2 tsp paprika
- 1 tbsp butter
- 1/4 tsp black pepper
- 1/4 tsp garlic powder
- 1/4 tsp dried rosemary
- 1/4 tsp salt

Directions:

1. In a small bowl, combine butter, black pepper, garlic powder, rosemary, thyme, paprika, and salt.
2. Rub chicken with butter spice herb mixture and place into the air fryer basket.
3. Cook at 375 F for 25 minutes.
4. Serve and enjoy.

Per serving: Calories: 325kcal; Fat: 15g; Carbs: 0.7g; Protein: 41g

117. Simple Spice Chicken Wings

Preparation time: 10 minutes

Cooking time: 30 minutes

Servings: 3

Ingredients:

- 1 1/2 lbs. chicken wings
- 1 tbsp baking powder, gluten-free
- 1/2 tsp onion powder
- 1/2 tsp garlic powder
- 1/2 tsp smoked paprika
- 1 tbsp olive oil
- 1/2 tsp pepper
- 1/4 tsp sea salt

Directions:

1. Add chicken wings and oil to a large mixing bowl and toss well.
2. Mix remaining ingredients and sprinkle over chicken wings and toss to coat.

3. Spray the air fryer basket with cooking spray.

4. Add chicken wings to air fryer basket and cook at 400 F for 15 minutes. Toss well.

5. Turn chicken wings to another side and cook for 15 minutes more.

6. Serve and enjoy.

Per serving: Calories: 280kcal; Fat: 19g; Carbs: 2g; Protein: 22g

118. Crispy Pork Chops

Preparation time: 10 minutes

Cooking time: 20 minutes

Servings: 4

Ingredients:

- 4 pork chops, boneless
- 2 eggs, lightly beaten
- 1 cup almond flour
- 1/4 cup parmesan cheese, grated
- 1 tbsp onion powder
- 1/2 tbsp garlic powder
- 1/2 tbsp pepper
- 1/2 tsp sea salt

Directions:

1. Preheat the air fryer to 350 F.

2. Spray the air fryer basket with cooking spray.

3. Mix almond flour, parmesan cheese, onion powder, garlic powder, pepper, and salt in a bowl.

4. Whisk eggs in a shallow bowl.

5. Dip pork chops into the egg, coat with almond mixture, and place into the air fryer basket.

6. Cook pork chops for 10 minutes. Turn pork chops to another side and cook for 10 minutes more.

7. Serve and enjoy.

Per serving: Calories: 450kcal; Fat: 35g; Carbs: 9g; Protein: 28g

119. Lemon Pepper Chicken Wings

Preparation time: 10 minutes

Cooking time: 16 minutes

Servings: 4

Ingredients:

- 1 lb. chicken wings
- 1 tsp lemon pepper
- 1 tbsp olive oil
- 1 tsp salt

Directions:

1. Add chicken wings into the large mixing bowl.

2. Add remaining ingredients over chicken and toss well to coat.

3. Bring chicken wings in the air fryer basket.

4. Cook chicken wings for 8 minutes at 400 F.

5. Turn chicken wings to another side and cook for 8 minutes more.

6. Serve and enjoy.

Per serving: Calories: 247kcal; Fat: 11g; Carbs: 0.3g; Protein: 32g

120. Dried Herbs Lamb Chops

Preparation time: 10 minutes

Cooking time: 20 minutes

Servings: 4

Ingredients:

- 1 lb. lamb chops
- 1 tsp oregano
- 1 tsp thyme
- 1 tsp rosemary
- 2 tbsp fresh lemon juice
- 2 tbsp olive oil
- 1 tsp coriander
- 1/4 tsp pepper
- 1 tsp salt

Directions:

1. Add all ingredients except lamb chops into the zip-lock bag.
2. Add lamb chops to the bag. Seal the bag, shake it well, and place it in the fridge overnight.
3. Place marinated lamb chops into the air fryer.
4. Cook at 390 F for 3 minutes. Turn lamb chops to another side and cook for 4 minutes more.
5. Serve and enjoy.

Per serving: Calories: 275kcal; Fat: 16g; Carbs: 1g; Protein: 30g

121. Asian Beef

Preparation time: 10 minutes

Cooking time: 20 minutes

Servings: 4

Ingredients:

- 1 lb. beef tips, sliced
- 1/4 cup green onion, chopped
- 2 tbsp garlic, minced
- 2 tbsp sesame oil
- 1 tbsp fish sauce
- 2 tbsp coconut aminos
- 1 tsp xanthan gum
- 2 red chili peppers, sliced
- 2 tbsp water
- 1 tbsp ginger, sliced

Directions:

1. Spray the air fryer basket with cooking spray.
2. Toss beef and xanthan gum together.
3. Add beef into the air fryer basket and cook at 390F for 20 minutes. Toss halfway through.
4. Meanwhile, add the remaining ingredients except for the green onion and heat over low heat in a saucepan.
5. When sauce begins to boil then, remove from heat.
6. Add cooked meat into the saucepan and stir to coat. Let sit in for 5 minutes.
7. Garnish with green onion and serve.

Per serving: Calories: 295kcal; Fat: 15g; Carbs: 6g; Protein: 35g

122. Delicious Cheeseburgers

Preparation time: 10 minutes
Cooking time: 12 minutes
Servings: 4
Ingredients:
- 1 lb ground beef
- 4 cheddar cheese slices
- 1/2 tsp Italian seasoning
- Pepper
- Salt

Directions:
1. Spray the air fryer basket with cooking spray.
2. Mix ground beef, Italian seasoning, pepper, and salt in a bowl.
3. Make four equal patties from meat mixture shapes and place them into the air fryer basket.
4. Cook at 375 F for 5 minutes. Turn the patties to another side and cook for 5 minutes more.
5. Place cheese slices on top of each patty, then cook for 2 minutes more.
6. Serve and enjoy.

Per serving: Calories: 325kcal; Fat: 16.5g; Carbs: 0.4g; Protein: 41.4g

123. Lemon Mustard Lamb Chops

Preparation time: 10 minutes
Cooking time: 15 minutes
Servings: 4
Ingredients:
- 8 lamb chops
- 1 tbsp lemon juice
- 1 tsp tarragon
- 1/2 tsp olive oil
- 2 tbsp Dijon mustard
- Pepper
- Salt

Directions:
1. Preheat the air fryer to 390 F.
2. Mix mustard, lemon juice, tarragon, and olive oil in a small bowl.
3. Brush mustard mixture over lamb chops.
4. Place lamb chops in an air fryer basket and cook for 15 minutes. Turn halfway through.
5. Serve and enjoy.

Per serving: Calories: 328kcal; Fat: 13.4g; Carbs: 0.6g; Protein: 48.1g

124. Garlic Thyme Pork Chops

Preparation time: 10 minutes
Cooking time: 15 minutes
Servings: 8
Ingredients:
- 8 pork chops, boneless
- 5 garlic cloves, minced
- 1 cup parmesan cheese
- 2 tbsp butter, melted
- 1 tsp thyme
- 1 tbsp parsley
- 2 tbsp coconut oil
- 1/4 tsp pepper
- 1/2 tsp sea salt

Directions:
1. Preheat the air fryer to 400 F.
2. Spray the air fryer basket with cooking spray.

3. Mix butter, spices, cheese, and coconut oil in a bowl.

4. Rub butter mixture on pork chops and place into the air fryer basket.

5. Cook for 10 minutes. Turn to another side and cook for 10 minutes more.

6. Serve and enjoy.

Per serving: Calories: 355kcal; Fat: 29g; Carbs: 2g; Protein: 23g

125. Asian Flavors Beef Broccoli

Preparation time: 10 minutes

Cooking time: 15 minutes

Servings: 3

Ingredients:

- 1/2 lb. steak, cut into strips
- 1 tsp garlic, minced
- 1 tsp ginger, minced
- 2 tbsp sesame oil
- 2 tbsp soy sauce
- 4 tbsp oyster sauce
- 1 lb broccoli florets
- 1 tbsp sesame seeds, toasted

Directions:

1. Add all ingredients except sesame seeds into the large mixing bowl and toss well—place bowl in the refrigerator for 1 hour.

2. Add marinated steak and broccoli into the air fryer basket and cook at 350 F for 15 minutes.

3. Shake the basket 2-3 times while cooking.

4. Garnish with sesame seeds and serve.

Per serving: Calories: 265kcal; Fat: 14g; Carbs: 12.5g; Protein: 21g

126. Easy Beef Broccoli

Preparation time: 10 minutes

Cooking time: 10 minutes

Servings: 4

Ingredients:

- 1 lb. round beef cubes
- 1/2 medium onion, diced
- 1 tbsp Worcestershire sauce
- 1/2 lb. broccoli florets, steamed
- 1 tsp olive oil
- 1 tsp onion powder
- 1 tsp garlic powder
- Pepper
- Salt

Directions:

1. Spray the air fryer basket with cooking spray.

2. Add all ingredients except broccoli into the large bowl and toss well.

3. Add bowl mixture into the air fryer basket and cook at 360 F for 10 minutes.

4. Serve with broccoli, and enjoy.

Per serving: Calories: 230kcal; Fat: 5g; Carbs: 7g; Protein: 36g

127. Juicy Rib Eye Steak

Preparation time: 10 minutes

Cooking time: 14 minutes

Servings: 2

Ingredients:

- 2 medium rib-eye steaks

- 1/4 tsp garlic powder
- 1/4 tsp onion powder
- 1 tsp olive oil
- Pepper
- Salt

Directions:

1. Coat steaks with oil and season with garlic powder, onion powder, pepper, and salt.
2. Preheat the air fryer to 400 F.
3. Place steaks into the air fryer basket and cook for 14 minutes. Turn halfway through.
4. Serve and enjoy.

Per serving: Calories: 469kcal; Fat: 31g; Carbs: 3g; Protein: 44g

128. Stuffed Pork Chops

Preparation time: 10 minutes

Cooking time: 28 minutes

Servings: 4

Ingredients:

- 4 pork chops, boneless and thick-cut
- 2 tbsp olives, chopped
- 2 tbsp sun-dried tomatoes, chopped
- 1/2 cup feta cheese, crumbled
- 2 garlic cloves, minced
- 2 tbsp fresh parsley, chopped

Directions:

1. Preheat the air fryer to 350 F.
2. Combine feta cheese, garlic, parsley, olives, and sun-dried tomatoes in a bowl.
3. Stuff the cheese mixture with all the pork chops.
4. Season pork chops with pepper and salt and place into the air fryer basket.
5. Cook for 28 minutes.
6. Serve and enjoy.

Per serving: Calories: 314kcal; Fat: 10g; Carbs: 2g; Protein: 19g

129. Lamb Meatballs

Preparation time: 10 minutes

Cooking time: 14 minutes

Servings: 8

Ingredients:

- 1 egg, lightly beaten
- 1 lb. ground lamb
- ¼ tsp bay leaf, crushed
- 1 tsp ground coriander
- ¼ tsp cayenne pepper
- ¼ tsp turmeric
- 1 onion, chopped
- 2 garlic cloves, minced
- ¼ tsp pepper
- 1 tsp salt

Directions:

1. Preheat the air fryer to 400 F.
2. Spray the air fryer basket with cooking spray.
3. Place all ingredients into the huge bowl, then mix until well combined.
4. Make small balls from the meat mixture, place them into the air fryer basket, and cook for 14 minutes. Shake the basket twice while cooking.
5. Serve and enjoy.

Per serving: Calories: 121kcal; Fat: 4g; Carbs: 2g; Protein: 16g

130. Flavorful Pork Tenderloin

Preparation time: 10 minutes

Cooking time: 15 minutes

Servings: 3

Ingredients:

- 1 lb pork tenderloin
- 1 tbsp vinegar
- 2 garlic cloves, minced
- 3 tbsp butter
- ½ tsp onion powder
- ½ tsp garlic powder
- ½ tsp cinnamon
- 1 tsp sage
- ½ tsp saffron

Directions:

1. Mix saffron, onion powder, garlic powder, cinnamon, and sage in a small bowl.
2. Rub pork tenderloin with the saffron mixture.
3. Now rub pork tenderloin with garlic and vinegar and sit for 10 minutes.
4. Preheat the air fryer to 320 F.
5. Place pork tenderloin into the air fryer and top with butter.
6. Cook for 15 minutes.
7. Slice and serve.

Per serving: Calories: 327kcal; Fat: 16g; Carbs: 2g; Protein: 40g

Desserts

131. Blueberry Muffins

Preparation time: 10 minutes

Cooking time: 20 minutes

Servings: 12

Ingredients:

- 3 large eggs
- 1/3 cup coconut oil, melted
- 1 1/2 tsp gluten-free baking powder
- 1/2 cup erythritol
- 2 1/2 cups almond flour
- 3/4 cup blueberries
- 1/2 tsp vanilla
- 1/3 cup unsweetened almond milk

Directions:

1. Preheat the air fryer to 325 F.
2. In a huge bowl, stir together almond flour, baking powder, and erythritol.
3. Mix in the coconut oil, vanilla, eggs, and almond milk. Add blueberries and fold well.
4. Pour batter into the silicone muffin molds and place into the air fryer basket in batches.
5. Cook muffins for 20 minutes.
6. Serve and enjoy.

Per serving: Calories: 215kcal; Fat: 19g; Carbs: 5g; Protein: 7g

132. Brownie Bites

Preparation time: 10 minutes

Cooking time: 12 minutes

Servings: 16

Ingredients:

- ¾ cup almond flour
- ½ tsp vanilla
- 2 eggs
- ½ cup unsweetened cocoa powder
- ¾ cup swerve
- 4 tbsp butter, melted
- Pinch of salt

Directions:

1. Preheat the air fryer to 325 F.
2. Whisk together butter, vanilla, eggs, cocoa powder, sweetener, and salt in a bowl.
3. Add almond flour and stir to combine.
4. Pour batter into the mini silicone molds and place into the air fryer.
5. Cook for 12 minutes or until done.
6. Serve and enjoy.

Per serving: Calories: 48kcal; Fat: 4.5g; Carbs: 1.9g; Protein: 1.5g

133. Pumpkin Muffins

Preparation time: 10 minutes

Cooking time: 20 minutes

Servings: 10

Ingredients:

- 4 large eggs
- 1/2 cup pumpkin puree
- 1 tbsp pumpkin pie spice
- 1 tbsp baking powder, gluten-free
- 2/3 cup erythritol

- 1 tsp vanilla
- 1/3 cup coconut oil, melted
- 1/2 cup almond flour
- 1/2 cup coconut flour
- 1/2 tsp sea salt

Directions:

1. Preheat the air fryer to 325 F.

2. In a huge bowl, stir together coconut flour, pumpkin pie spice, baking powder, erythritol, almond flour, and sea salt.

3. Stir in eggs, vanilla, coconut oil, and pumpkin puree until well combined.

4. Pour batter into the silicone muffin molds and place into the air fryer basket in batches.

5. Cook muffins for 20 minutes.

6. Serve and enjoy.

Per serving: Calories: 150kcal; Fat: 13g; Carbs: 7g; Protein: 5g

134. Easy Cheesecake

Preparation time: 10 minutes

Cooking time: 10 minutes

Servings: 6

Ingredients:

- 2 eggs
- 16 oz cream cheese, softened
- 2 tbsp sour cream
- 1/2 tsp fresh lemon juice
- 1 tsp vanilla
- 3/4 cup erythritol

Directions:

1. Preheat the air fryer to 350 F.

2. Add eggs, lemon juice, vanilla, and sweetener to a large bowl and beat with a hand mixer until smooth.

3. Add cream cheese & sour cream, then beat until fluffy.

4. Pour batter into the two four-inch spring-form pans, place in an air fryer basket, and cook for 8-10minutes at 350 F.

5. Remove from the air fryer and let it cool completely.

6. Place in refrigerator overnight.

7. Serve and enjoy.

Per serving: Calories: 296kcal; Fat: 28g; Carbs: 2.4g; Protein: 7.7g

135. Choco Chips Cookies

Preparation time: 10 minutes

Cooking time: 15 minutes

Servings: 4

Ingredients:

- 1 egg
- 3 tbsp butter
- 1 tsp vanilla
- ¼ tsp baking powder
- 2 tbsp macadamia nuts, crushed
- 1 cup almond flour
- 2 tbsp unsweetened chocolate chips
- Pinch of salt

Directions:

1. In a bowl, beat the egg using a hand mixer.

2. Add almond flour, butter, vanilla, baking powder, and salt and stir well.

3. Add Chocó chips and macadamia nuts and mix until dough is formed.

4. Preheat the air fryer to 360 F.

5. Make cookies from the dough, place them into the air fryer, and cook for 15 minutes.

6. Serve and enjoy.

Per serving: Calories: 215kcal; Fat: 20g; Carbs: 4.5g; Protein: 4g

136. Delicious Spiced Apples

Preparation time: 10 minutes
Cooking time: 10 minutes
Servings: 6
Ingredients:

- 4 small apples, sliced
- 1 tsp apple pie spice
- 1/2 cup erythritol
- 2 tbsp coconut oil, melted

Directions:

1. Add apple slices in a mixing bowl, sprinkle sweetener, apple pie spice, and coconut oil over the apple, and toss to coat.

2. Transfer apple slices in air fryer dish. Place dish in air fryer basket and cook at 350 F for 10 minutes.

3. Serve and enjoy.

Per serving: Calories: 73kcal; Fat: 4.6g; Carbs: 8.2g; Protein: 0g

137. Coconut Pie

Preparation time: 10 minutes
Cooking time: 12 minutes
Servings: 6
Ingredients:

- 2 eggs
- 1/2 cup coconut flour
- 1/2 cup erythritol
- 1 cup shredded coconut
- 1 1/2 tsp vanilla
- 1/4 cup butter
- 1 1/2 cups coconut milk

Directions:

1. Place all ingredients into the huge bowl, then mix until well combined.

2. Spray a 6-inch baking dish with cooking spray.

3. Pour batter into the prepared dish and place in the air fryer basket.

4. Cook at 350 F for 10-12 minutes.

5. Slice and serve.

Per serving: Calories: 282kcal; Fat: 28.9g; Carbs: 6.3g; Protein: 4g

138. Strawberry Muffins

Preparation time: 10 minutes
Cooking time: 15 minutes
Servings: 12
Ingredients:

- 3 eggs
- 1 tsp ground cinnamon
- 2 tsp baking powder

- 2 1/2 cups almond flour
- 2/3 cup fresh strawberries, diced
- 1/3 cup heavy cream
- 1 tsp vanilla
- 1/2 cup Swerve
- 5 tbsp butter

Directions:

1. Preheat the air fryer to 325 F.
2. Add butter and sweetener in a bowl and beat using a hand mixer until smooth.
3. Add eggs, cream, and vanilla and beat until frothy.
4. Sift almond flour, cinnamon, baking powder, and salt in another bowl.
5. Add almond flour mixture to wet ingredients and mix until well combined.
6. Add strawberries and fold well.
7. Pour batter into the silicone muffin molds and place into the air fryer basket in batches.
8. Cook muffins for 15 minutes.
9. Serve and enjoy.

Per serving: Calories: 205kcal; Fat: 18g; Carbs: 6g; Protein: 6g

139. Cream Cheese Muffins

Preparation time: 10 minutes
Cooking time: 16 minutes
Servings: 10
Ingredients:

- 2 eggs
- 1/2 cup erythritol
- 8 oz cream cheese
- 1 tsp ground cinnamon
- 1/2 tsp vanilla

Directions:

1. Preheat the air fryer to 325 F.
2. Mix cream cheese, vanilla, erythritol, and eggs in a bowl until soft.
3. Pour batter into the silicone muffin molds and sprinkle cinnamon on top.
4. Place muffin molds into the air fryer basket and cook for 16 minutes.
5. Serve and enjoy.

Per serving: Calories: 90kcal; Fat: 8.8g; Carbs: 13g; Protein: 2.8g

140. Almond Coconut Cheese Muffins

Preparation time: 10 mins
Cooking time: 10 mins
Servings: 8
Ingredients:

- 1 egg
- 1 tsp. baking soda
- 1 cup almond flour
- 2 tbsps. coconut flakes
- 2 tsps. erythritol
- 1 tsp. vinegar
- 1 cup cream cheese
- Tweak of salt

Directions:

1. Beat cream cheese and egg in a bowl until well combined.

2. Include almond flour, vinegar, baking soda, coconut flakes, sweetener, and salt and beat till thoroughly mixed.

3. Preheat the air fryer to 360 F.

4. Pour batter into silicone muffin molds and place into the air fryer.

5. Cook for ten mins.

6. Serve and enjoy.

Per serving: Calories: 134kcal; Fat: 12g; Carbs: 1g; Protein: 3.7g

141. Fluffy Butter Cake

Preparation time: 10 mins

Cooking time: 35 mins

Servings: 8

Ingredients:

- 6 egg yolks
- 3 cups almond flour
- 2 tsp. vanilla
- 1 egg, lightly beaten
- ¼ cup erythritol
- 1 cup butter
- Pinch of salt

Directions:

1. Preheat the air fryer to 350 F.

2. In a bowl, beat butter and sweetener until fluffy.

3. Include vanilla and egg yolks and beat until well combined.

4. Include remaining ingredients and beat until combined.

5. Pour batter into the air fryer cake pan and place into the air fryer, and cook for thirty-five mins.

6. Slice and serve.

Per serving: Calories: 315kcal; Fat: 32g; Carbs: 2g; Protein: 5g

142. Delicious Vanilla Custard

Preparation time: 10 mins

Cooking time: 20 mins

Servings: 2

Ingredients:

- 5 eggs
- 2 tbsps. swerve
- 1 tsp. vanilla
- ½ cup unsweetened almond milk
- ½ cup cream cheese

Directions:

1. Add eggs to a bowl and beat using a hand mixer.

2. Include cream cheese, sweetener, vanilla, and almond milk and beat for a further two mins.

3. Spray two ramekins with cooking spray.

4. Pour batter into the prepared ramekins.

5. Preheat the air fryer to 350 F.

6. Put ramekins into the air fryer and cook for twenty mins.

7. Serve and enjoy.

Per serving: Calories: 381kcal; Fat: 32g; Carbs: 5g; Protein: 18g

143. Berry Cobbler

Preparation time: 10 mins

Cooking time: 10 mins

Servings: 6

Ingredients:

- 1 egg, lightly beaten
- 1 tbsp. butter, melted
- 2 tsps. swerve
- ½ tsp. vanilla
- 1 cup almond flour
- ½ cup raspberries, cut
- ½ cup strawberries, cut

Directions:

1. Preheat the air fryer to 360 F.
2. Add sliced strawberries and raspberries to the air fryer baking dish.
3. Sprinkle sweetener over berries.
4. Mix almond flour, vanilla, and butter in the bowl.
5. Add egg to almond flour mixture and stir well to combine.
6. Spread almond flour mixture over sliced berries. Cover the dish with foil, put it into the air fryer and cook for ten mins.
7. Serve and enjoy.

Per serving: Calories: 66kcal; Fat: 5g; Carbs: 3g; Protein: 2g

144. Cappuccino Muffins

Preparation time: 10 mins

Cooking time: 20 mins

Servings: 12

Ingredients:

- 4 eggs
- 2 cups almond flour
- 1/2 tsp. vanilla
- 1 tsp. espresso powder
- 1/2 cup sour cream
- 1 tsp. cinnamon
- 2 tsps. baking powder
- 1/4 cup coconut flour
- 1/2 cup Swerve
- 1/4 tsp. salt

Directions:

1. Preheat the air fryer to 325 F.
2. Include sour cream, vanilla, espresso powder, and eggs in a blender and mix till smooth.
3. Include almond flour, cinnamon, baking powder, coconut flour, sweetener, and salt. Mix again till homogenous.
4. Pour batter into the silicone muffin molds and place into the air fryer basket. (Cook in batches)
5. Cook muffins for twenty mins.
6. Serve and enjoy.

Per serving: Calories: 150kcal; Fat: 13g; Carbs: 5.3g; Protein: 6g

145. Almond Bars

Preparation time: 10 mins
Cooking time: 35 mins
Servings: 12
Ingredients:
- 2 eggs, lightly beaten
- 1 cup erythritol
- ½ tsp. vanilla
- ¼ cup water
- ½ cup softened butter
- ¾ cup cherries, pitted
- 1 ½ cup almond flour
- 1 tbsp. xanthan gum
- ½ tsp. salt

Directions:
1. Mix almond flour, erythritol, eggs, vanilla, butter, and salt in a container till the dough is formed.
2. Press dough in the air fryer baking dish.
3. Place in the air fryer, then cook at 375 F for ten mins.
4. Meanwhile, mix cherries, xanthan gum, and water.
5. Pour cherry mix over cooked dough and cook for a further twenty-five mins.
6. Slice and serve.

Per serving: Calories: 168kcal; Fat: 15g; Carbs: 5g; Protein: 4g

146. Cinnamon Apple Chips

Preparation time: 10 mins
Cooking time: 8 mins
Servings: 6
Ingredients:
- 3 Granny Smith apples, wash, core and thinly slice
- 1 tsp. ground cinnamon
- Tweak of salt

Directions:
1. Rub apple slices with cinnamon and salt and place them into the air fryer basket.
2. Cook at 390 F for eight mins. Turn midway completely.
3. Serve and have fun with it.

Per serving: Calories: 41kcal; Fat: 0g; Carbs: 11g; Protein: 0g

147. Moist Cinnamon Muffins

Preparation time: 10 minutes
Cooking time: 12 minutes
Servings: 20
Ingredients:
- 1 tbsp. cinnamon
- 1 tsp. baking powder
- 2 scoops vanilla protein powder
- 1/2 cup almond flour
- 1/2 cup coconut oil
- 1/2 cup pumpkin puree
- 1/2 cup almond butter

Directions:
1. Preheat the air fryer to 325 F.

2. In a big container, mix all dry components and mix thoroughly.

3. Include wet components to the dry ingredients and mix until well combined.

4. Pour batter into the silicone muffin molds and place into the air fryer basket. (Cook in batches)

5. Cook muffins for twelve mins.

6. Serve and enjoy.

Per serving: Calories: 80kcal; Fat: 7.1g; Carbs: 1g; Protein: 3g

148. Chocolate Soufflé

Preparation time: 10 mins

Cooking time: 12 mins

Servings: 6

Ingredients:

- 3 eggs separated
- 1 tsp. vanilla
- ¼ cup swerve
- 5 tbsps. butter, melted
- 2 tbsps. heavy cream
- 2 tbsps. almond flour
- 2 oz. dark chocolate, melted

Directions:

1. Mix melted chocolate and butter.

2. In a bowl, whisk egg yolk with sweetener until combined.

3. Include almond flour, heavy cream, and vanilla and whisk completely.

4. Inside a separate container, whisk egg whites till soft peaks form.

5. Include the egg white to the chocolate mix slowly and fold completely.

6. Pour the chocolate mixture into the ramekins and place them into the air fryer.

7. Cook at 330 F for twelve mins.

8. Serve and enjoy.

Per serving: Calories: 240kcal; Fat: 21g; Carbs: 8g; Protein: 5g

149. Easy Lava Cake

Preparation time: 10 mins

Cooking time: 9 mins

Servings: 2

Ingredients:

- 1 egg
- 1/2 tsp. baking powder
- 1 tbsp. coconut oil, melted
- 1 tbsp. flax meal
- 2 tbsps. erythritol
- 2 tbsps. water
- 2 tbsps. unsweetened cocoa powder
- Tweak of salt

Directions:

1. Whisk all ingredients into the bowl and transfer to two ramekins.

2. Preheat the air fryer to 350 F.

3. Place ramekins in an air fryer basket and bake for 8-9 minutes.

4. Carefully remove ramekins from the air fryer and let it cool for 10 minutes.

5. Serve and enjoy.

Per serving: Calories: 119kcal; Fat: 11g; Carbs: 4g; Protein: 5g

150. Cashew Pie

Preparation time: 10 mins
Cooking time: 18 mins
Servings: 8
Ingredients:

- 1 egg
- 2 oz. cashews, crushed
- ½ tsp. baking soda
- 1/3 cup heavy cream
- 1 oz. dark chocolate, melted
- 1 tbsp. butter
- 1 tsp. vinegar
- 1 cup coconut flour

Directions:

1. Include egg to a container and beat using a hand mixer. Include coconut flour and mix thoroughly.
2. Include butter, vinegar, baking soda, heavy cream, and melted chocolate and stir thoroughly.
3. Include cashews and mix thoroughly.
4. Preheat the air fryer to 350 F.
5. Include prepared dough to the air fryer baking dish and flatten it into a pie shape.
6. Cook for eighteen mins.
7. Slice and serve.

Per serving: Calories: 105kcal; Fat: 8g; Carbs: 5g; Protein: 2.4g

30-Day Meal Plan

Days	Breakfast	Lunch	Dinner	Dessert
1	Perfect Breakfast Frittata	Flavorful Fried Chicken	Lemon Butter Salmon	Choco Chips Cookies
2	Healthy Mix Vegetables	Tilapia Fish Fillets	Cheesy & Juicy Pork Chops	Strawberry Muffins
3	Asparagus Frittata	Easy Bacon Shrimp	Quick & Easy Steak	Cappuccino Muffins
4	Perfect Breakfast Frittata	Tasty Pork Bites	Delicious White Fish	Moist Cinnamon Muffins
5	Spinach Egg Breakfast	Pork With Mushrooms	Perfect Salmon Fillets	Fluffy Butter Cake
6	Breakfast Egg Muffins	Garlic Mayo Shrimp	Dried Herbs Lamb Chops	Cinnamon Apple Chips
7	Spinach Muffins	Air Fried Catfish	Delicious Whole Chicken	Easy Lava Cake
8	Zucchini Salad	Garlic Thyme Pork Chops	Cajun Cheese Shrimp	Almond Coconut Cheese Muffins
9	Cheese Stuff Peppers	Simple Spice Chicken Wings	Shrimp With Veggie	Blueberry Muffins
10	Broccoli Stuffed Peppers	Parmesan Walnut Salmon	Crispy Pork Chops	Pumpkin Muffins
11	Egg Cups	Chili Garlic Shrimp	Asian Flavors Beef Broccoli	Delicious Spiced Apples
12	Roasted Pepper Salad	Delicious Cheeseburgers	Almond Coconut Shrimp	Cream Cheese Muffins
13	Spinach Frittata	Flavorful Pork Tenderloin	Delicious Crab Cakes	Delicious Vanilla Custard

14	Omelet Frittata	Air Fried King Prawns	Easy Beef Broccoli	Chocolate Soufflé
15	Simple Egg Soufflé	Lemon Chili Salmon	Lemon Pepper Chicken Wings	Easy Cheesecake
16	Bacon Egg Muffins	Simple Air Fryer Steak	Spicy Shrimp	Brownie Bites
17	Scrambled Eggs	Lemon Mustard Lamb Chops	Herb Chicken Roast	Coconut Pie
18	Indian Cauliflower	Cheese Crust Salmon	Basil Parmesan Shrimp	Berry Cobbler
19	Healthy Squash	Beef Roast	Mediterranean Chicken	Almond Bars
20	Zucchini Muffins	Creamy Shrimp	Curried Drumsticks	Cashew Pie
21	Broccoli Muffins	Juicy Rib Eye Steak	Nutritious Salmon	Cinnamon Apple Chips
22	Perfect Breakfast Frittata	Spicy Prawns	Pork Strips	Easy Lava Cake
23	Spinach Egg Breakfast	Cajun Shrimp	Asian Beef	Almond Coconut Cheese Muffins
24	Breakfast Egg Muffins	Lamb Meatballs	Fish Packets	Choco Chips Cookies
25	Cheese Stuff Peppers	Stuffed Pork Chops	Cheesy Crab Dip	Strawberry Muffins
26	Broccoli Stuffed Peppers	Pesto Salmon	Moist Lamb Roast	Cappuccino Muffins
27	Egg Cups	Miso Fish	Lamb Rack	Moist Cinnamon Muffins
28	Perfect Breakfast Frittata	Steak Fajitas	Tuna Patties	Delicious Spiced Apples

| 29 | Healthy Mix Vegetables | Italian Seasoned Chicken Tenders | Salmon Patties | Cream Cheese Muffins |
| 30 | Asparagus Frittata | Creamy Crab Dip | Thai Shrimp | Delicious Vanilla Custard |

Conversion Chart

Volume Equivalents (Liquid)

US Standard	US Standard (ounces)	Metric (approximate)
2 tablespoons	1 fl. oz.	30 mL
¼ cup	2 fl. oz.	60 mL
½ cup	4 fl. oz.	120 mL
1 cup	8 fl. oz.	240 mL
1½ cups	12 fl. oz.	355 mL
2 cups or 1 pint	16 fl. oz.	475 mL
4 cups or 1 quart	32 fl. oz.	1 L
1 gallon	128 fl. oz.	4 L

Volume Equivalents (Dry)

US Standard	Metric (approximate)
⅛ teaspoon	0.5 mL
¼ teaspoon	1 mL
½ teaspoon	2 mL
¾ teaspoon	4 mL
1 teaspoon	5 mL
1 tablespoon	15 mL
¼ cup	59 mL
⅓ cup	79 mL
½ cup	118 mL
⅔ cup	156 mL
¾ cup	177 mL
1 cup	235 mL

2 cups or 1 pint	475 mL
3 cups	700 mL
4 cups or 1 quart	1 L

Oven Temperatures

Fahrenheit (F)	Celsius (C) (approximate)
250°F	120°C
300°F	150°C
325°F	165°C
350°F	180°C
375°F	190°C
400°F	200°C
425°F	220°C
450°F	230°C

Weight Equivalents

US Standard	Metric (approximate)
1 tablespoon	15 g
½ ounce	15 g
1 ounce	30 g
2 ounces	60 g
4 ounces	115 g
8 ounces	225 g
12 ounces	340 g
16 ounces or 1 pound	455 g

Conclusion

It may seem like rhetoric, but an air fryer is a dream machine. An air fryer is a kitchen counter power tool that utilizes convective heat transfer to cook food by circulating hot air (as well as, in some circumstances, oil). Many models have a range of two to six liters and cost $70 – $200 based on the model.

Fried foods have an irresistible flavor and feel. There's nothing quite like biting into a crispy French fry and fried chicken just to be embraced by a melting yet tender core.

We all understand that processed, fried foods cannot be a regular part of our diet. This is where an air fryer helps a lot. With little to no oil, this equipment creates crisp, juicy, and delicious foods. Fried chicken, French fries, quesadillas, donuts, egg rolls, seafood, and tater tots will all be made without using trans fats by using an air fryer.

Air frying is generally better than cooking in oil. It reduces calories by about 70% – 80% and covers much less fat. This cooking process can decrease any of the other adverse repercussions of oil frying. When you fried potatoes and other starchy foods, the chemical acrylamide is created, which has been related to an enlarged danger of cancer in studies. According to one report, air frying reduces the volume of acrylamide in French fries by 90%.

The batter consumes the oil used to fry the meal. Fried foods retain their pleasing crunch on the exterior while remaining crispy on the inside. Foods that have been fried have a beautiful, dark color that is attractive to the eye. Air-fried items have the same conventional texture and taste as properly fried foods but are guilt-free.

However, the air fryer is capable of even more. In contrast to fried foods, you can use your air fryer for baking, barbecuing, steaming, & roasting foods in far less time than you can with conventional techniques. With the air fryer, you can cook risotto, stir-fries, pizzas, sauces, and desserts promptly and with a stellar performance.

Printed by Libri Plureos GmbH in Hamburg, Germany